THE TOILET ON THE SIDEWALK

THE TOILET
on the
SIDEWALK

finding hope in Christ
through unexpected circumstances

LIANE K. HENKELL

ISBN: 979-8-218452-37-7

Cover and Book design: Kristen Schade

Cover art: Based on AI-generated images using Adobe FireFly.

To my gracious God,
from whom all blessings flow

Contents

Preface ix

A Pile of Rocks 1

The Toilet on the Sidewalk. 4

Great Expectations 7

Plain and Simple 10

Dichotomous 13

Living Brokenhearted. 16

Unfinished 19

Rocks in My Shoes 22

Lessons from a Cactus 26

Stop the Ride...I Wanna Get Off!. 29

Running without a Finish Line 33

The Happiest Place. 37

Letting Go 41

The Saving Power of Red Liquid 44

Prayer Changes Things: Part I. 48

Prayer Changes Things: Part II 51

Jesus Is My Pool Boy. 55

To Infinity...and Beyond 59

Moving Forward 63

Worth the Wait. 66

Steps of Grace 69

Surrendering the Pen 72

Deleting the Comma 76

When It's Not Always Well 80

What I Didn't Deserve 85

A Mary Christmas to You 90

Butterfly Skin 93

The Cone of Shame 97

My Waze vs. God's Waze 100

Shared Custody 104

There's No Place like Home 108

Unknown 112

How Much Longer??? 117

Traditiooooon......TRADITION! 122

This Too Shall Pass 125

Clothed in Anxiety 129

Perpetually Saturday 133

The Recliner on the Sidewalk 137

Alterations 141

The Saxophone on the Sidewalk 145

You Have to Go through It 148

Acknowledgments 153

Preface

There is a good chance that if you have gone through some type of hardship in your life, whether infertility or divorce or a medical diagnosis or even a loved one's death, it was preceded by hope. Hope that maybe this was the month you would get pregnant. Hope that maybe you and your spouse could reconcile. Hope that perhaps the doctor's diagnosis was wrong and there was still a long life ahead. Hope that maybe death wasn't imminent.

I remember nearly eight years ago desperately clinging to hope. Hope that my fourteen-year-old son would regain consciousness after I witnessed his UTV accident. Hope that once I reached him and started CPR, he would start breathing again. Hope that once the paramedics arrived, they'd be able to fix what was broken. Hope that once we got to the hospital, it would all be okay.

But we never made it to the hospital. Or even to the helicopter that was waiting to take us there. Instead my hope ended on a tarmac in the eastern Arizona mountains when I heard the words every mother hopes she'll never hear: "I'm sorry ma'am. We did all we could."

Hope was shattered in that very second on the morning of September 5, 2016. Surely this could not be my reality. Where was hope now?

Perhaps you, too, are shaking your head with where life's journey has taken you. How could this be? This wasn't how it was supposed to turn out! Like me, maybe you're wondering where hope even fits into your life now. Being thrust into a new reality you didn't expect can leave you hopeless. Angry. Devastated. Numb. Confused. And did I mention hopeless?

I will never claim to be an expert on loss. I don't hold any professional degrees in psychology or counseling. I did not pour over books on grief and loss after my son died, because my heart and mind were too overwhelmed.

But this I know as a child of God: hope is not lost. On the other side of pain and loss is a new hope. A *different* hope. Not a hope that merely *wishes* life could be what it used to or a hope that crosses its fingers, but a hope that is expectant, giving us a reason to get up each day, put our feet on the floor, and continue to live. Hope might have died the day Jesus hung on a cross, but it also rose again three days later.

Hope in Christ means trusting that one day, God will make all things new. He will wipe every tear from our eyes. He will restore what has been lost. It may not be on this side of the grave, but He is faithful to continually renew our hope each day. Not because we are owed it or because He feels sorry for us. But because He is love. He is hope. I know it, because I have lived it each day since September 5, 2016.

I pray these devotionals convey the hope I have in Christ as His child. And the hope God desires for you to have, too. It is this very hope that saw me through my darkest days of grief. And it's that same hope that continues to sustain me even to this very day. May *His* words, not mine, bring you that same hope for whatever unexpected journey you find yourself on today.

A Pile of Rocks

"My help comes from the Lord, the Maker of heaven and earth."

~ Psalm 121:1

There is no more daunting task for a teacher than having to pack up a classroom she's lived in for several years. But that's exactly where I found myself in May of 2022. Every drawer, cabinet, and shelf was filled with…stuff. A lot of stuff was tossed out. Some stuff was saved for the next teacher. But the stuff that had value or purpose (to me) got packed in boxes to be put in a storage unit. I remember one of the last things I packed was a small tower of rocks that had been hot glued together. I had received it a few years prior, not from a student, but from a friend, who had also suffered a devastating loss. Not of a child, but of a spouse.

When he gave it to me, he asked, "Do you know what an Ebenezer is?" I vaguely recalled something from the Bible about rocks and an old hymn about raising an Ebenezer. I kept my mouth shut, not wanting to admit that phrase conjured images of holding up a miniature Ebenezer Scrooge in a Lion King-esque type moment. He said, "After the Israelites defeated the Philistines in battle, Samuel set up a pile of rocks to remind the people never to forget that God had helped them in their victory. And every time God's people would look at these rocks, this "Ebenezer" as it was called, they could remember that God had met them there." He continued, "Your writings are like that for so many. They are a living testament to how God has helped you. They are your Ebenezer."

I have kept that pile of rocks on my desk every day since, to remind me of all I had endured. Miscarriages, divorce, single parenting, custody battles, the death of my son...but it wasn't that those rocks represented the *hardships*, but rather the *help of God* in those hardships. When I looked at the rocks, my heart remembered:

> In the pain of my three miscarriages, I remembered the comfort my heavenly Father provided.

> In the despair of watching my husband walk away from our 15-year marriage, I remember that God was my constant companion and provider.

> In the exhaustion of single parenting, I remember God had given me strength for each new day.

> In the anxiety of being in court and before judges, I remember the peace of God flooding my heart and keeping me steady.

> In the agony of watching my son die, I remember the assurance God gave me that Joe was with Him forever.

But in the sorrow of visiting my son's grave, I am reminded that the stone that bears his name and the years of his life is a tangible Ebenezer. This "rock" of remembrance tells what God has done: He gave my son life on this earth and made him His child through the waters of baptism. It also tells what He *will* do on the last day: raise all believers to new life in Christ.

There are other stones. Other hurts in my life. But for each one, there is also a remembrance of God's faithfulness and promise of hope.

And that's exactly what this book is.

It's about all those stones piled up. Not for people to look at them and say, "That poor girl. Look at all she's been through!" But to say, "That incredible God! Look at all He's brought her through."

Many of these devotions were written out of the overwhelming pain and grief of losing a child. But they were also written out of the simultaneous comfort and hope found in Christ in the midst of that pain and grief. They might have started as an outlet for me to release all those thoughts and feelings that were bottled up and needed processing. But ultimately, they were written for you, sweet reader. They were written to point you to Christ and to the hope and assurance of salvation found only in Him. They were written to help you look past the temporal and focus on the eternal. They were written to show you how in real and tangible ways where my help comes from. And where your help comes from, too.

So here it is...my Ebenezer. Which was oddly enough inspired by a toilet on the sidewalk.

The Toilet on the Sidewalk

"Let us run with perseverance the race marked out for us,
fixing our eyes on Jesus, the Author and Perfecter of faith."

~ Hebrews 12:1

It was a night like any other. Except it wasn't. Because nothing was the same anymore. It was a night of trying to adjust to a new normal, which never would really be normal again.

It was a month after Joe died, and I was trying to get into the habit of going for a short walk after dinner. I knew exercise was good, almost necessary for me. And it was hard to be in the house with pictures and memories. I needed time to process the day, reflect on life, cope with this new reality that had been thrown at me. It was also my time to spend alone with God and connect with Him. I plugged the tangled headphones into my iPhone, found my favorite Pandora station and set off around the block. As I settled into my reflective gait, my head was down, always looking just at the two or three feet in front of me. And perhaps that's why I didn't see it coming until I was nearly upon it.

A toilet. Directly in front of me. Blocking my path.

It wasn't off to the side in the grass. It wasn't facing away from me. It was dead center in the middle of the sidewalk, as if it were looking straight at me. Staring me down. Challenging me. Mocking me. Daring me to pass. Interrupting my perfectly peaceful walk of solitude.

I remained unmoving, staring at that toilet for a while. I had seen a lot of odd things in my low-income neighborhood over the months:

mattresses piled in the yard, broken chairs, dilapidated couches, outdated TVs on the edge of the lawn, even a larger-than-life green and white-striped chair next to a wooden moose. But a toilet? And let alone, one blocking my path? It was absolutely ridiculous!

And yet, here I was, frozen. My eyes transfixed on this newest eyesore of the block. I must have stood there for a good minute just looking in disbelief at what was in front of me.

I did eventually step to the side and pass that toilet. I mean, what choice did I have? To stare at it all night? That would be a waste of time. To turn around and go back? That wouldn't really accomplish my goal of continuing my peaceful walk, would it? I had to pass it to get on with what I set out to do.

As I stood there, transfixed by the toilet, it hit me.

Life had thrown me for a loop. It had put me on a path I never wanted to walk. And for lack of a better analogy, it had placed a toilet on the sidewalk. It was certainly not what I had expected and it was the last thing I had wanted. I had truly experienced the ultimate crap (or whatever word you'd prefer to use) of life. My 14-year-old baby boy was gone. In an instant. A mother's worst nightmare realized.

And I was faced with a choice: I could stay frozen in my path, focusing on the horrors of my son's death. Heaven knows I've relived it in my mind more times than I care to say. I could turn around and turn my back on the path God chose for me. Or I could step to the side and continue to walk. Continue to worship. Continue on the path with God towards the destination to which He has called me.

I'd venture to guess that you, too, have had a "toilet on the sidewalk" moment in your life. Something you didn't see coming, something you didn't plan on happening. Something you wish was different in life. And maybe it stopped you in your tracks. Perhaps you didn't even know how you would be able to move on from the shock. If so, you and I are in good company.

And had it been up to me, to rely on my strength alone, I'm pretty sure I'd still be stuck on that sidewalk, staring at the toilet. But fortunately, my story didn't end there. And neither does yours. The only way we can continue to move forward on this path of life is to do exactly what Paul described in Hebrews 12:1. Instead of fixating on the things of this world, we can "fix our eyes on Jesus" because of the miraculous strength and comfort that He pours into our hearts. He's done it for me. And He will do it for you. With His strength inside of you, you can keep fighting the fight and running the race. And if you're walking or even limping, that's okay, too.

We may not know what's ahead on the path, but we can trust in the sovereignty of God. We can trust in HIS power. HIS grace. HIS strength. HIS plan. Take your eyes off that toilet and put them on God. He knows the path. He sees what's ahead. He's making a way. He's already there. And even when it feels like there's no good that can come from it, God will make something beautiful out of our sidewalk toilets.

PRAYER

Lord, there are difficult trials in my life I didn't see coming. Sometimes it's hard to come to terms with my current reality. But you are still good. And you are still faithful. And you are sovereign over it all. Give me Your strength to help me keep fighting the fight and moving forward in Your plans for my life, despite the toilets I encounter on the sidewalk. Keep my eyes fixed on You. Bring something beautiful out of my ashes for Your glory alone. Amen.

REFLECTION

What "toilet on the sidewalk" moments have you experienced? How have you seen God's faithfulness in these moments?

_____

_____

_____

_____

_____

Great Expectations

"Come, thou long expected Jesus, born to set Thy people free
From our fears and sins release us, let us find our rest in Thee
Israel's strength and consolation, Hope to all the earth Thou art
Dear desire of ev'ry nation, joy of ev'ry longing heart!"

~ Charles Wesley, 1744

If you had asked me on Christmas Day, 2015 what I thought I'd be doing on Christmas Day, 2016, I wouldn't have guessed that going to the cemetery would be one of them. Or that I'd be picking out a Merry Christmas balloon for my son's grave. But there I was that morning, with said balloon in hand. At the cemetery. On a chilly Christmas morning. Alone.

Every Christmas, I always looked back to the year before and marveled at how far God had brought the kids and me. I would look forward with expectation to the next Christmas to see where God would take us. And hope that the brokenness of years past would somehow be redeemed.

It wasn't so long ago that Christmas was filled with church services, children excited for presents to open, and the busyness of being a family of four. Then 2012 came and left me reeling when my husband walked away from our 15-year marriage. It wasn't at all what I expected. Christmas changed. Children were now shared. Holidays were split. New memories and traditions had to be formed.

And then 2016…a year of unbelievable, unbearable and most certainly unexpected loss. Loss that left me gasping for air some days. Loss that didn't want to look back to last year, because there was joy in waking up with my kids on Christmas morning. Loss that didn't want to look ahead, because maybe next Christmas would be worse. This was not how I expected life would turn out.

Not only was *my* Christmas one of unexpectation, but so was that first Christmas. There were angel sightings, a teenage virgin impregnated by the Holy Spirit, lowly shepherds being the first to hear the news, and a crude barn for the King of Kings to name a few. Yet, people had been expecting Jesus for literally thousands of years! So what was the big surprise? Perhaps He just didn't come the way people expected He would. But what the *people* expected didn't play into this first Christmas. It was the *Father's* plan. All of it, down to the last detail. No surprises, perfectly executed by the God of creation.

As I stood there at the cemetery on Christmas morning, I thought about the life I expected for my son and the plans God had for him. Why wasn't he supposed to live beyond fourteen years? Couldn't there have been a different outcome? Was Joe's death part of God's plan?

To answer those questions, I needed to go back to where it all began. No, not with my son's birth, but with *God's* son's birth. Why did Jesus need to be born at Christmas all those years ago? As I contemplated the answer, there was only one conclusion I could draw: Death was never a part of God's plan when He created the world. He created a perfect earth. However, our world didn't stay perfect, nor did our created bodies. We do not make perfect choices. Nor do those around us. That has been the reality of the world since the Garden of Eden.

And because of this, God created a new plan so we could be saved from our sin and once again, live in a perfect world. It's literally what Jesus' name means: *God saves*. God redeemed the plan through His Son, so that one day we could be part of a new world where death will be no more. A world that my son now gets to be a part of forever. And that one day, I will, too.

I would venture to guess that you, too, have wondered about God's plan for someone you love. Or maybe even yourself. And when life didn't turn how you expected, you became angry at God for His supposed "plan", which seemed anything but perfect. But friends, know this: pain, sickness, heartbreak, separation, death…those things are not and will never be a part of God's plan. But He can redeem those awful things to point people to His one and only plan accomplished by His one and only Son.

That accomplished plan gives hope to those who grieve. To bring peace to those whose life didn't turn out the way they thought. And even comfort to those who bring a balloon to their son's grave on a chilly Christmas morning.

So now we, like the people of Israel did long ago, wait with great expectation that Jesus will come again as He promised. Maybe like me, that longing is deep in your heart, especially on difficult holidays full of loss. We don't know what we can expect next year or the year after or really any day we live on this earth. But we can expect this: comfort in our sorrow, rest for our troubled hearts, forgiveness from our sins, and hope of life eternal. All because a baby was born on Christmas Day.

PRAYER

Lord, life didn't turn out the way I expected. The plans for my life and for those I love are difficult to accept. Help me recognize that Your plans are to heal, to restore, and to bring us closer to Your side. I'm so grateful that your plan in sending Jesus, although unexpected to many, was absolutely perfect. There was no other way to be saved other than through the death of Your Son on the cross. Thank you for that incredible gift of salvation and life eternal with You! Amen.

REFLECTION

How does God's gift of His Son bring comfort to you in times when your reality doesn't meet your expectations?

_____

_____

_____

_____

_____

Plain and Simple

For a handful of weeks after Joe passed away, people took care of us by bringing over meals just about every day. Our refrigerator was well-stocked with meatballs, chicken, salads, rice, and dinner rolls a-plenty. It seemed a little silly that I only had one other person to care for, yet I needed food brought to my door each day. But I quickly learned that things that once seemed so simple and effortless were made extremely challenging by grief. Taking a shower was a chore, getting dressed was laborious, and running a simple errand overwhelmed me. The simple was somehow made very difficult.

But while those tasks may seem easy to some, those of you who have been in the trenches of grief and loss get it. Every day becomes a day of survival. You're asked to do so many difficult things that thinking beyond "the next thing" isn't mentally possible. The grief itself is so overwhelming that it takes everything in you to take the simple steps. And the difficult ones, too.

Some of the hardest steps I had to take were actual steps. After making arrangements at the funeral home, I had requested to be with Joe's body one final time. The director graciously set up a private room for me to be in, even though he explained my son would be covered with a quilt. As I walked into that empty parlor room, I knew I had done many hard things in my life, but this one would just about top the list.

"Just take the next step," I told myself over and over again. I forced my feet to keep moving until I crossed the room. Kneeling on the floor beside Joe's body, I laid a hand on top of the quilt. Tears began to pour down my face. As I was on my knees, crying out to God for strength to bear this terrible burden, I looked up. There on the wall above where Joe's body lay hung a cross. Just a few inches tall, made on a nondescript wood. No embellishments, no details. Plain and simple.

I had seen hundreds of crosses in my lifetime, heard many sermons about the cross and sung countless songs with the word "cross" in them. But it wasn't until this moment that the power of the cross became overwhelmingly significant, personal, and dare I say... simplistic. It was for times like these, when the blow of death leaves us shattered, that the cross—or rather the work of Jesus on the cross — was incredibly necessary. It was accomplished so that ultimately, death wouldn't have the final say. The cross meant death for Jesus, but it meant *life* for those who believe. It might seem ridiculous to those who don't think the cross means anything. But for the believer...the cross means *everything*.

Don't get me wrong: there was nothing "simplistic" or easy about the steps Jesus took to get to the cross. Each one was excruciating, back-breaking, agonizing. But each difficult step taken was for you. For me. And each step Jesus took closer to the cross meant you would never have to put one foot in the grave. You don't need a degree in theology or need to study the Scriptures intensely to understand the simplicity of the cross.

Jesus died so you wouldn't have to. Jesus rose so you could rise, too.

Grief and loss make our lives complicated and difficult. But the cross makes it easier to bear. It gives us hope. It provides comfort. It allows peace.

As I walked out of that funeral parlor, the tears still flowed. Life was still hard. My heart was still shattered. But I knew that wouldn't be the last time I would be with my son. I had the hope of heaven in my future. I was comforted by the resurrection to come. I had the peace and assurance of eternal life in my heart.

Plain and simple.

PRAYER

Lord, with all the difficulties and complexities in this life, I am thankful for the simplicity of the cross. I know there wasn't anything easy about the death You died, but I am so grateful that Your love for me held You there. As I walk through this life, help me with those challenging steps I take, as well as the simple ones, too. I know there is never a step I take that I don't need You by my side. Amen.

REFLECTION

Are there times when you have dismissed the power of the cross? What does the cross mean to you today?

_____

_____

_____

_____

_____

Dichotomous

*"Brothers and sisters, we do not want you to be uninformed about those
who sleep in death, so that you do not grieve like the rest of mankind,
who have no hope. For we believe that Jesus died and rose again, and so we
believe that God will bring with Jesus those who have fallen asleep in him."*

~ 1 Thessalonians 4:13-14

There are a handful of words I love to say just for the sake of
hearing them. Words that make me feel smart when they
roll off my tongue. Onomatopoeia. Monotonous. Discombobulate.
Octogenarian. Antidisestablishmentarianism. But my favorite, as of
late, isn't quite as long as that.

Dichotomous.

Working with young children, I don't get to use that word as often
as I'd like. However, it's one I've found to be particularly relevant when
it comes to describing what it's like walking through this journey of
grief. To most outside observers, it would appear that I'm surviving
just fine. But there is an inner struggle of polar opposite feelings on a
daily, sometimes hourly basis.

There is overwhelming sadness when I look at the empty pas-
senger seat beside me as I'm driving, wishing there was once again a
14-year-old boy constantly changing the radio station. And yet, there
is overwhelming joy when I think about that same boy singing with
the saints around the throne of God. There's anxiety each morning
when I wake up and wonder how I'll even get dressed and survive
another day. But as I manage a classroom of children with calmness
and patience, I can feel God's spirit of peace present. Then there's
the long term. I don't know how long I'll have to live on this earth
before I'll see my son again. And some days, that thought is almost

paralyzing. Almost. But then God fills me with hope and longing for the coming of His Son again like I never have felt before.

Sadness and joy. Anxiety and peace. Despair and hope. The first part offered by the world. The second part offered by Christ.

This dichotomous concept is even evident on social media. I've joined a small handful of Facebook groups for grieving parents—some are Christian, some are not. And let me tell you, there is a marked difference between these two groups. The posts in the non-Christian groups contained an abundance of anger, sadness, despair, grief, and hopelessness. People would share how months and even years after their child died, they were still mad at the reality of their situation - and perhaps even at God. They still were so paralyzed by sadness that they couldn't get out of bed. They cried constantly with no end in sight. I became fearful and wondered if this was really all I had to look forward to in this journey of grief.

But the posts in the groups specifically for Christians, had a very different tone. Were there feelings of sadness and pain and anger? Absolutely. The situation these grieving parents found themselves in was terrible and awful and devastating...but it didn't end there. There was more. Whether it was in the encouragement in the comments made, or in the belief that there was more to their child's life than what this world offered, the difference was clear.

HOPE.

There was hope because of the belief in the life, death, and resurrection of Jesus. You see, for those of us who know these things to be true, hopelessness is not part of the equation. Our hope, as Paul describes, looks different than the world's hope. Sadness is temporary. Anger is fleeting. Despair doesn't last forever. What does last is the result of hope: peace, comfort, and yes, even joy. If there was no hope that there was life after death for our loved ones or for us, we surely would not be able to walk through this life. It's hope that puts our feet on the floor to walk through another day.

Because hope is not merely a wish. It's believing in the promises of God as absolute truth.

A few months after my son died, my daughter and I were back in the Midwest visiting my sister. We went to a nearby park to exercise and preliminarily (now *that's* a fun word, too) burn off some New Year's Eve calories. It was thrilling for us desert folk to see so many leaves on the ground, albeit brown and dead. I loved watching Ella's smiling face as she crunched through those leaves in her boots. And as she grabbed a handful of them and flung them into the air, I couldn't help but think of that word: dichotomous. Here we were, surrounded by dead leaves and bare trees, and yet experiencing great joy in the midst of it.

That perfectly sums up the journey of grief for the believer. We've been consumed by our loss. We are surrounded by sadness. We walk in the midst of it every day. But there are moments of joy in the journey. Moments where we take what's been given us and throw our hands up in praise to our Creator, knowing the leaves won't always be brown. The branches won't always be bare. And although it appears to be dead, there is still life in the tree, waiting to burst forth when a new season comes. We rejoice in that truth. That promise. That HOPE.

PRAYER

Lord, I praise You that even in the midst of my trials You still give me joy despite my sadness, peace despite my anxiety and hope despite my despair. I know that one day, there will be an end to my earthly struggles because of the promise of eternal life. Help me to encourage others in their trials with the same hope I've received from You. Amen.

REFLECTION

What conflicting emotions have you experienced recently?
How does hope play a part in which emotion dominates?

Living Brokenhearted

"The Lord is close to the brokenhearted
and saves those who are crushed in spirit."

~ Psalm 34:18

Ten years ago, I walked into a room at a local church, signed my name to the roster, and sat down at an empty table. I didn't know anyone, which was how I preferred it. I didn't even really want to be there, but deep down I knew I needed to be. DivorceCare class. It was one of those surreal moments you find yourself in and completely overwhelmed by. This was a class for other people. Surely not me.

I was still in a great deal of shock over what had transpired just weeks prior. My husband and best friend of over fifteen years and dad to our two children dropped a bombshell. He had had multiple affairs over the course of many years. And he was filing for divorce. As a result, he would also need to leave the church at which he was the senior pastor. I never saw it coming.

As I sat at the table looking around at the other weary, distraught faces around me, my eyes wandered to the whiteboard in the front of the room. The instructor had written a Bible verse on the board. You guessed it. The one at the beginning of this devotion.

I wasn't sure how I had lived over thirty-seven years of life not being aware of that verse. Maybe I hadn't really needed it until now. Tears immediately began to fill my eyes, because if there ever was a description of me, this was it. Brokenhearted. Crushed in spirit.

That verse became very personal to me over the years. It not only brought me comfort, but it was a verse I often shared with others who were going through challenging times. And it's no wonder that this passage was one I clung to in the wake of my son's death. I mean, if there was ever a time to feel brokenhearted, this was definitely it, right? But as I had my Bible open to this very verse, my eyes locked in on "brokenhearted" and "crushed in spirit," as it had so many times. I closed my eyes and whispered, "God. I am so weary from being these things far too often." And in the stillness, God whispered back, "This verse isn't about *you*. Look what *I* am doing!" I opened my eyes and read with fresh eyes.

THE LORD IS CLOSE. HE SAVES.

It was like being hit with a spiritual two by four. The focus of this passage was not about *my* current emotional state, but about God and *His* action. *His* movement towards me. *His* love and desire to save me.

How many times have we had the spotlight on ourselves and our own suffering instead of what God is doing in the midst of it? If you're anything like me, it's far too often. Even when my heart is broken for those around me—and there are so many walking through the darkest of valleys—I tend to focus on their state of grief and sadness, instead of what the Lord might be doing.

But, friends, let me encourage you today as much as I encourage myself with these words. We have a God who sees our broken hearts and our crushed spirits. And He doesn't sit by idly. He moves closer. When I felt like I lost my best friend, Jesus filled that void and was always there to listen. When I was worried about financially supporting my children, He stepped in as my provider. When I felt like no one loved me, Scripture was there to remind me how much I was loved by the God of the universe. When anxiety took over in those late nights alone, my Father reminded me of His promise to never leave my side.

My heart was still broken. And maybe yours is, too. What the world has thrown us is anything but easy. And those crushed spirits? As much as we'd like to acknowledge that phrase with a resounding, "Amen!," that word "crushed" actually translates to the word "contrite" or sorry. Maybe we resonate to that one, too…especially when we put the focus all on us, instead of on the One who can heal our broken hearts. Fortunately, our crushed spirits are not the end of our story. God loved us so incredibly much that He sent His Son to save us, so that by His grace, we would not have to live brokenhearted forever. Our contrite hearts will be made whole again in the presence of our Savior. Eternally.

So do not read the words of the psalmist and weep. Read them and rejoice! "The Lord is close to the brokenhearted and saves those who are crushed in spirit."

PRAYER

Lord, while some might distance themselves from me and the brokenness I find myself in, You never do. Instead you come near and stay with me through the pain. Forgive me when I've made my situation all about me and my suffering, instead of You and Your goodness. You are so good, Lord! Thank you for sending Jesus to save me, so that I would have the hope that one day, my tears will be no more in Your presence. Amen.

REFLECTION

Which words of Psalm 34:18 are you drawn to? What is God doing in the midst of your suffering?

_____

_____

_____

_____

_____

Unfinished

"You saw me before I was born. Every day of my life was recorded in your book. Every moment was laid out before a single day had passed."

~ Psalm 139:16

W hen my son entered "big kid school," my mother gave me a picture frame with multiple cut-outs to showcase each of his school pictures from Kindergarten to his senior year of high school. I can remember when there was just one photo in that frame and it seemed like a lifetime until it would be filled with pictures. The years went by and more pictures were added. I loved looking at that frame and seeing how my sweet boy had grown each year. I'd read the familiar verse in the center of the frame from Jeremiah 29:11 and pray about the plans God had for Joseph. I couldn't wait to put in that final senior picture and see what God was going to do with his life! And then September 5th, 2016 happened.

The plan was left incomplete. Unfinished.

It is an incredibly difficult thing to accept that your child is no longer a part of your present. But it's an equally difficult thing to acknowledge that your child will not be a part of your future. I had plans for my child, as I'm sure all parents do. Joe was smart, driven, and hard-working, and I knew those traits would serve him well in his career someday. I longed to see him graduate and tell him how proud I was of him, knowing all the sacrifice it took to get to that moment. I imagined the day I would dance with him at his wedding and invite a new daughter into the family. I dreamed about the day I would hold his son or daughter for the first time and beam with pride as a grandmother. All of those things were wonderful things to dream about.

But it took quite some time to come to the harsh reality that those were *my* plans. Not God's.

I'm reminded of that each time I visit the cemetery. Buried next to my Joe is little Hannah Grace who died when she was two days old. Just a few spots down is another little girl who died of cancer before she turned six. Andrew is nearby and didn't quite make it to his fourteenth birthday. All seemingly too young and leaving a life unfinished. So many plans left undone.

It's a difficult concept to think that God's plans just might include a life ending too early, isn't it? I don't know about you, but it's one that I struggle with on a daily basis. One that I have questioned God about more times than I care to admit. One that often produces moments of doubt and confusion. And one that seemingly demands a most extraordinary amount of faith and trust in a still-loving and faithful God.

We know that death is the result of living in a sinful, fallen world. There are accidents, there are choices people make, there are bodies that just don't work perfectly. We get that. But then we wonder why God didn't intervene. If He *could* have saved my loved one, then why didn't He? Can't God do anything? Even the impossible? Yes, He can. But also consider these important truths:

God sees the big picture. HE has the plan, not us with our limited perspective.

Our loved one's life was exactly as long as God meant it to be. There is nothing we could have done to extend it, even by a second.

Job 14:5 confirms this when he says,

"You have decided the length of our lives. You know how many months we will live, and we are not given a minute longer."

It is on days we doubt God's plan, or feel guilty that maybe we should have done something differently to change the outcome, that we need to hear these words the most.

God *did* have a plan for Joe. And for your loved one, too. Even though it wasn't what you and I would have chosen, it was still the most beautiful plan ever imagined. It's the same plan He has for you and me. It's one full of hope and a future that began from the beginning of the world and was completed when Christ breathed the words, "It is finished." Because it was then that the plan of sacrifice, redemption, and love was complete. And that plan means that my son *is* a part of my future.

For those who have gone before, their plan is complete. Their race is done. Their victory has been won. It's the rest of us still here on earth who aren't done yet. Our race is unfinished. God has more to do in and through us. But while we wait, we can confidently declare with Job these powerful words of hope:

"I know that my Redeemer lives, and that in the end he will stand on the earth. And after my skin has been destroyed, yet in my flesh I will see God."
~ Job 19:25–26

PRAYER

Lord, I may not always understand the "whys" of this life. Help me trust that Your plans and Your ways are higher than mine. You see everything and You know everything. You saw our sin and our brokenness and You knew there was only one plan that would lead us to life eternal. Thank you for Jesus' finished work on the cross. May that give me hope and strength for each new day, until I am with You forever. Amen.

REFLECTION

What has been "unfinished" in your life? How does knowing that God has a "plan" bring you comfort in trials?

The Rocks in My Shoes

*"So now I am glad to boast about my weaknesses, so that the power of Christ
can work through me. That's why I take pleasure in my weaknesses, and in
the insults, hardships, persecutions, and troubles that I suffer for Christ.
For when I am weak, then I am strong."*

~ 2 Corinthians 12:9b–10

I f there's one thing you should know about hiking in the South-
western desert, it's this: trails are *rocky*. (And it's important to
have an ample water supply, so I suppose two things.) Sometimes
the rocks are big, sometimes they're small, sometimes they're boul-
ders but sometimes they're itty bitty little rocks. And invariably, no
matter how tightly I tie my hiking boots or how thick a sock I wear,
one of these teeny tiny little rocks will end up in my shoe. It's like the
Murphy's law of hiking.

For the record, I never start off with a rock in my shoe. In fact, the
first few minutes on the trail are usually quite pleasant and rock-free.
But once that itty bitty rock finds its way into my hiking boot, I begin
to step right on it. And it HURTS. I try to shift my foot around and
move the rock. I really don't want to stop on the trail, untie the shoe,
dump out the rock and retie my laces. Besides, there's no place to sit
down—not until I reach the top of the mountain. I have no choice but
to keep going. But then a second tiny rock joins the first one. More
shaking my foot. More shifting my toes around to adjust the rocks.
More realization that those rocks aren't going anywhere. As I continue to hike, I begin to get seriously annoyed. How did these rocks
get there? Why *my* shoe? Hadn't I stayed on the trail? The journey to
the top was hard enough without these dumb rocks!

Annoying as those rocks were, I began to think about how much our life's journey is a lot like hiking with rocks in our shoe.

Perhaps your life's journey started off just fine...maybe it was even pleasant in the beginning. You had lots of energy and optimistic goals. But then rocks began to creep in as the journey continued...small rocks like job changes and parenting frustrations and living on a tight budget. But maybe there were big rocks, too. Miscarriages. Infertility. Divorce. A cancer diagnosis. Addiction. The death of someone you dearly loved. (that one's more like a boulder.) When those rocks came, there might not have been any warning. You wondered how you even ended up with these rocks, when you had stayed on the path, had your shoes on tight, and even had your Jesus music playing through your earbuds. Maybe the rocks were so painful that you just wanted to sit down, stop moving, take the rocks out and give up.

If you're nodding along to any of this, know that I have been there. More than once. Many times I have pleaded with God to take away the rocks in my shoe. And more and more I identify with Paul when he begged God to take away the metaphorical thorn in his flesh (or rock in his shoe) that was given to him. But God says to him, what He also says to you and me:

> *"My grace is all you need. My power works best in weakness."*
> ~ 2 Corinthians 12:9a

I don't know about you, but all these rocks in my shoes make me weak. But it is in *our* very weakness that the Lord shows *His* strength and power through us. Which makes Paul's words a fitting response:

> *"So now I am glad to boast about my weaknesses, so that the power of Christ can work through me. That's why I take pleasure in my weaknesses, and in the insults, hardships, persecutions, and troubles that I suffer for Christ. For when I am weak, then I am strong."*
> ~ 2 Corinthians 12:9b–10

As much as it's tempting to put our focus on the rocks in our shoes that weaken us, Paul's encouragement and example is that we put our focus on The Rock that strengthens us. Those itty bitty rocks, and perhaps even the big ones, lose their hold on us when we look to our Lord and Savior, our Rock. And *this* Rock isn't one of annoyance, discomfort or pain, but rather is described as our fortress, our deliverer, our redeemer, and *our salvation*. Perhaps it's fitting then, that the rock that was rolled away from the tomb on that Easter morning was a guarantee that death had been conquered on our behalf and there would be no rock in our shoe big enough to separate us from the love of our True Rock.

Until we are reunited with our Rock, it's inevitable that we will continue on our journey with rocks in our shoes. Sometimes those rocks might shift enough so we can barely feel them. Consider these moments of refreshment as a gift from God. It's okay to laugh and love life at those times, despite the rocks in your shoes. And sometimes those rocks might cause much pain and discomfort. It's then that God puts people on the path with you to share the pain they, too, have walked through as an encouragement and hope to your heart. Maybe God might even put someone on the trail who has similar rocks in their shoes that you can encourage along the way.

But one thing I know: God *will* give us the strength to make it to the end of the journey. Rocks and all. Can you imagine the relief we'll feel when Jesus stoops down to untie our dusty hiking boots and dump all those rocks out? I imagine we'll be running barefoot on the perfect paved streets of gold. With not a rock in sight.

PRAYER

Lord, sometimes the rocks in my shoes are too painful for me to walk. I am reminded far too often of the trials on life's trail and lose focus. Remind me that You are my Rock—and the rock You moved from the entrance of the tomb on the day of Your resurrection changed everything. It gives me hope that one day these smaller rocks will be a distant memory in the light of Your presence. Strengthen me on my journey until I reach the rockless streets of gold. Amen.

REFLECTION

What "rocks" are present in your shoes? How is God's strength on display in your life despite the rocks?

_____

_____

_____

_____

_____

Lessons from a Cactus

"Or do you not realize about yourselves that Jesus Christ is in you?"

~ 2 Corinthians 13:5

I'm a girl who was raised in the Midwest—rural Nebraska to be exact. I grew up with a backdrop of corn fields and silos and flat land for as far as the eye could see. So it's no wonder that even after living in the desert for over twenty years, I'm still fascinated with its landscape. There are some who don't think there's much beauty to be seen in the desert, but I absolutely love it. Especially when it's spring-time…little flowers of purple and yellow dot the sides of hiking trails, the landscape seems relatively green, and there's a buzzing of insects all around. (Alright, so that part I could live without.)

There's no shortage of trails to hike around the Valley and when spring break arrived, I finally had some time to try out a new trail. Normally I'm not one to take photographs when I hike, but finding myself particularly drawn to the enormity of the Saguaro cacti on the trail, I channeled my inner tourist. Every hundred feet or so, I'd find myself digging out my phone for another breathtaking shot of the towering plants.

From a distance, these majestic cacti seem like they would be awe-inspiring. But if you've ever been close enough to a Saguaro, you'll notice it often has several holes bored through the flesh from where various birds and desert creatures have made their homes. The base of the cactus has been eaten away from wild javelina and jackrabbits. Occasional wildfires char the base as well. Not only that, but the skin of the cactus is subject to sunburn and frostbite. So, how is it, after enduring all these things, the Saguaro is able to keep standing?

Because of what's *inside.*

Internally, the cactus is strong. There are long shafts of wooden ribs that run through the length of the cactus that are banded together to provide stability. The wood of large cactus species, such as the Saguaro, have a high fiber content, which means it is extremely sturdy. Not only that, but the average Saguaro can store over a thousand gallons of water in its ribs, which provide even more support.

That makes good sense for a cactus, but what about people? There are lots of us who might feel a bit like the outside of a Saguaro—full of holes, burnt, eaten up by the troubles of this world. Perhaps other people have demanded much of us or unexpected life events caused us to feel like we might not survive what it is we're dealing with. We've all gone through trials in life, whether big or small, and if we're blessed, we have good friends and family who come to our side to see us through and share words of comfort with us to let us know we're not alone. Words like, "God is with you" or "He's right beside you." And while those are perfectly accurate truths about God that can bring a measure of comfort, they stop short of the most wonderful, crucial truth to discover:

God isn't just *with* us. God is *within* us.

Many people marvel at how I've survived burying my four-teen-year-old son. They say, "You're so strong!" or "I could never be as strong as you!" Oh, friends. *Nothing* could be further from the truth! Yes, prayers have sustained me, music has spoken to my heart, hugs have brought me comfort. But how is it that I've been able to endure this trial, along with many others?

Because of *Who's* inside.

God *within* us is the reason we can still stand, despite what life throws our way. He is our day-to-day survival strategy. Like the long taproot of the Saguaro, our vertical taproot of faith dives deep into the soil of God's Word. We soak up the *Living Water* as He fills our hearts with peace and strength. We grow by spending time in prayer and worship. Our horizontal roots reach out to our family and friends for love, support, and comfort to hold us firmly in place. This is how we can survive those fires, bites, and extreme conditions that seek to devour us and our faith. So we can confidently stand and say with the apostle Paul,

> *"I am crucified with Christ; and it is no longer I who live,*
> *but it is Christ who lives in me."*
> ~ Galatians 2:20

I'm not sure about you, but knowing that truth makes me stand a whole lot taller. It puts fear in its place. It gives me joy on my saddest days, hope in my despair, comfort for my sorrow, and purpose for my pain. It empowers me to know that I have a living God who makes me, a plain girl from rural Nebraska, *His* dwelling place.

PRAYER

Lord, thank you for not only promising to be with me, but to live within me. It is Your strength and Your peace inside me that gives me the ability to bear my burdens and survive the troubles of this world. Give me opportunities to spend time in Your word, so that my parched soul can be refreshed. Provide people in my life who I can reach out to for comfort and support in my times of need. Amen.

REFLECTION

How does knowing that God is inside you impact your perspective on the difficulties you face? Who has God placed in your life for support? Consider sending them a message of thanks for being a source of encouragement to you.

_____

_____

_____

_____

_____

Stop the Ride...I Wanna Get Off!

"I cling to you; your right hand upholds me."

~ Psalm 63:8

Unbeknownst to me, the summer of 2016 would be the last summer vacation with both my children. As we were already planning to attend a family wedding, we decided to indulge our love of roller coasters and spend a day enjoying the thrill rides at Knott's Berry Farm. Research had been done on which rides were the craziest, had the shortest lines, and gave us the most bang for our buck. It was a glorious day of beautiful California weather, poor nutrition, and all the screaming our lungs could take. (Okay, so the screaming was mostly just me.) A running joke became my line of, "Is it too late to get off?" after we were strapped in for what was sure to be another wild ride. And my non-sympathetic children would just laugh and say, "Yep! Too bad, Mom!" So I'd hold on to that safety bar as tightly as I could and off we'd go, barreling down the track at high speeds, ready for the twists and turns and loop-de-loops. We left the park that day feeling exhausted, exhilarated, and extremely blessed for that time together as a family. Life was good.

But just a handful of weeks later, I found myself on a new ride I'd never been on: the roller coaster of child loss. It wasn't my choice to ride it and there was no getting off once it started. The world seemed to be spinning by, I felt turned upside down most days, and all the twists and turns made it hard to breathe. I prayed for the ride to be over soon, even though I knew it wasn't possible. And just when the ride would slow down a little, there would be a painful jolt that reminded me I was still on this roller coaster.

Going into my son's room was always one of those "painful jolts" of reality. The shirts hung in the closet, all cattywampus on the hangers. (That boy never could seem to hang a shirt properly.) The computer begged for Joe's fingers to be on the keys, playing Minecraft much longer than he should be. And then the bed...perfectly made, with no one to sleep under its covers. How I longed to tiptoe over to that bed, see my son's sweet face sound asleep, and pray over him as I would often do! It was too much. Too much pain. Too much missing. Too much emptiness in that room. In that wave of grief, my mouth opened and out came the words that had been weighing on my heart for far too long:

"Stop the ride, God! I wanna get off. I'm DONE! Done with being separated from my son! I'm ready for him to come back home."

You might not be on the roller coaster of child loss, but perhaps it's another type of ride you didn't choose to be on. Maybe it was someone else's choices that put you there and maybe it was even your choice to ride that ride. Or maybe it wasn't anyone's choice. But I'll venture to guess that there are days you are simply *done* with the ride you find yourself on. You want to bail. You wish the ride operator would put on the brake and stop the ride, so you could climb out and plant your feet firmly on the ground. And maybe, like me, you've just gotten so frustrated and disillusioned with being on the ride that you find yourself yelling at God.

It may be that God responded to you. But that wasn't the case for me. I'd love to say God spoke words of assurance to me in that moment. I would have settled for a small whisper to my heart. But not this time. There was only silence. Painful, aching silence.

I imagine when Jesus was on earth, He felt like getting off the roller coaster that would end at His death, too. In fact, the night before He died, He prayed in the Garden of Gethsemane for His Father to stop the ride so He could exit. "Dad. I'm done. I can't do what you want me to do. Let's forget this whole dying business. Tell me there's another way this can all go down." (I may have paraphrased that passage, but that's the gist.) And you know how God responded?

Me neither. That's because all four Gospels make no mention of God saying, "Sure, Son. I can see you've had enough. You're done. I'll find another way." Because He didn't. Truth be told, there is no record of God responding. Maybe He did and we just weren't privy to that conversation. But maybe...maybe there was a painful, aching silence.

The second part of Jesus' prayer that night was possibly the most important: "Yet not my will, but yours be done." (Luke 22:42) Jesus submitted to the will of His Father *over His own*. He wouldn't get off the ride unless God said He could. But God didn't. So Jesus had His answer: He would cling to His Father as tightly as He could and stay on the ride until death had been conquered. And He did just that... until God separated Himself from His Son moments before His death. All so that Jesus could experience the full consequence of sin for us. So that we would never have to be separated from God again.

And if He had chosen to get off the ride? We'd be lost. With no hope. No eternal future. No promise of being in the glorious presence of God someday. No chance to see those we love so dearly again. Like my sweet boy and countless others I know.

We don't always get to choose where this roller coaster of life will take us. We don't know when it will end. But we do have the assurance that God can be trusted and knows what He's doing. When life gets full of twists and turns and loop-de-loops, let's cling tightly to our Father. Maybe our white knuckles can relax a bit, because we can trust in the Operator to take us where He's planned for us to go on this side of eternity. We can also trust Him to bring us back to the safety of His loving arms, where the ride all began.

PRAYER

Lord, I didn't choose to be on this difficult roller coaster I find myself on, but I trust that You are still good and You are still in control. You even proved Your goodness and faithfulness to us on a path You didn't choose either—the cross. I am forever grateful You didn't get off that ride. Because of Your death and resurrection, I have hope that there is more to this life than the difficulties I face. Keep me close to You during this ride of life until I am home in heaven forever. Amen.

REFLECTION

Describe a roller coaster moment in your life. Express your thankfulness to Jesus for willingly staying on the ride all the way to the cross so that death could be no more.

_____

_____

_____

_____

_____

Running without a Finish Line

"Even youths grow tired and weary, and young men stumble and fall;
but those who hope in the Lord will renew their strength.
They will soar on wings like eagles; they will run and not grow weary,
they will walk and not be faint."

~ Isaiah 40:30–31

I have a lot of respect for people who run long distances. Or short distances for that matter. I decided to try to become one of those people a couple of years ago. You know, a person who actually enjoys running and is good at it? I didn't really have any strategy, except to run every day or two and try to run farther and longer than I did the previous day. As you can imagine, that didn't work out so well. Some days I couldn't go as far as I could the day before and I'd end up feeling defeated. Some days I had lots of energy to keep going and felt encouraged. At one point, I'm fairly certain I ran nearly two and a half miles without stopping. (A pretty amazing feat for someone who couldn't even run the half-mile in high school P.E. class.) But despite all my efforts, I never really figured out how people could run and not get that nagging cramp in their side. You know, the kind that feels like a sharp knife digging into your ribs every time you breathe? Or how does one maintain an energy level to run for such a long period of time? Even if I didn't get a side cramp, I couldn't seem to find the stamina to keep going.

I never did become a serious runner. But that didn't stop me from imagining what it would be like to run a 5K or 10K and actually cross a finish line. There would be something so rewarding, so exhilarating about taking that final step and declaring a personal victory, after knowing all the hard work I had put in. There'd be cheering and photo ops and let's not forget about the medal. Ah, yes…the finish line!

Life is full of finish lines, isn't it? We count down to the next paycheck, weekend, vacation, holiday, birthday, graduation, or anniversary, and think, "If I can just make it till…." And perhaps life is wonderful for that brief shining moment, until the reality of daily life sets in again.

I've mistakenly thought the same way about this journey of grief I find myself on. If I can just make it through this holiday or this anniversary or this milestone, I will have somehow reached the end. But if there's one reality I've learned, it's that there *is* no end. There is no day that I will ever wake up and say, "Well. I made it. Glad that's over!" Because it never is. It never will be. And that is a most wearying reality. It goes beyond physical, mental, and emotional exhaustion. It's life exhaustion.

It's like running without a finish line.

You may not be a runner, but it's possible that you, too, find yourself dealing with pain and brokenness in your life and wish there was a finish line. Maybe you've just started the race or maybe you've been running it for a long time. And let's be honest: "running" may not be the word you'd use. Perhaps it's more like "limping" with a constant cramp in your side. Sometimes the cramp is hardly noticeable. And other times, it seems to be all you can notice. You just want the pain to go away.

Surprisingly, the way to get rid of those nasty side cramps during difficult life journeys isn't dissimilar to what to do if you're *actually* running. According to running websites, personal blogs, and friends I know who run, the first thing to do is to *not panic*, or in other words, *do not fear*. Focus on breathing, slow down, stop if you need too. Use your hand to press on the part that hurts.

It's ironic how one also has to do that in grief as well. It might look different for you than for me, and that's okay. Everyone's journey is different, just as everyone processes grief differently. For a while, my anxiety was so out of control, I had to take medication to help.

I hiked and took long walks and practiced deep breathing. I listened to calm music and colored in coloring books. I took naps and rested, even when there was work to be done. But most importantly, I learned to show myself grace, because I just couldn't run at the pace I could before I started this journey.

But how about using my hand to press on the part that hurts? No medication or hiking trail or music or markers or breathing technique was going to do that. Rather, that's where God steps in, puts a gentle hand on our very weary and broken hearts and presses in with the truth of His Word.

"My soul is weary with sorrow; strengthen me according to your word."
~ Psalm 119:28

"I will refresh the weary and satisfy the faint."
~ Jeremiah 31:25

"Come to me, all you who are weary and burdened, and I will give you rest."
~ Matthew 11:28

"Yes, my soul, find rest in God: my hope comes from him."
~ Psalm 62:5

Those words don't automatically get rid of those nasty side cramps. They don't change the reality of the race we're running. But they do make it bearable by assuring us that God promises strength, rest, refreshment, and hope for our exhausted hearts when we just can't seem to take another step. He sends people to run the race with us and to be our cheering section by encouraging us to keep running this race. But best of all, He showed us grace by sending Jesus to run a perfect race on our behalf, so that one day, we will cross that finish line. *His* victory won through His own work on the cross becomes *our* victory as well.

While there may not be any photos taken at our races' end, I imagine there will be quite a bit of cheering from those who have finished the race. And even though there won't be any shiny medals to wear around our neck, there will be a crown of life placed on our heads. There will be Jesus' arms to rest in eternally after the race. May all those things encourage us to keep going, slow as it may be, until we reach the finish line of heaven!

PRAYER

Lord, I am so often weary from running this race. Strengthen me with Your presence. Revive me with Your Holy Spirit. Send people to cheer me on and give me the perseverance to finish this journey. When I feel like giving up, press the truth of Your word into my heart. May the race that You won for me encourage me each day until I reach Your arms in heaven. Amen.

REFLECTION

What encouragement could you use in your journey? How can you be an encouragement to those around you in their race as well?

_____

_____

_____

_____

_____

The Happiest Place

"There is more than enough room in my Father's home. If this were not so,
would I have told you that I am going to prepare a place for you?
When everything is ready, I will come and get you,
so that you will always be with me where I am."

~ John 14:2–3

As a little girl growing up in Southern California in the late 70s, I used to make frequent visits to "The Happiest Place on Earth" with my family. Disneyland was less than fifteen miles away from our home, and back in the day, one could simply park a car in the parking lot right in front of the entrance and walk into the park. If you came after 5 p.m., you didn't even need an admission ticket. You simply purchased books of tickets for individual rides. Which is exactly what my budget-conscious family did. However, our Disneyland trips weren't without some preparation. My dad would come home early from work, and my mom would have dinner ready by 4 p.m. She'd also pack a few little snacks to throw in her purse in case we got hungry after our fun adventures.

Going to Disneyland as a child was certainly memorable, but it was nothing compared to experiencing it as a parent. And as every parent knows, it's important to prepare your children for the trip by familiarizing them with songs, movies, and books filled with Disney characters, right? Being no exception to the rule, I dutifully made sure my three-year-old son was prepared for his first trip to "The Happiest Place on Earth." I'll never forget the squeals of delight as Joe flew through the skies on the Peter Pan ride, the wonder on his face as he rode "It's a Small World," the sound of his little voice belting out, "Heigh-Hooooo!," and the thrill of seeing his favorite Disney characters in person. After nine straight hours of fun, Joe finally fell asleep in the Tiki Room wrapped in his father's arms. All that preparation paid off.

There were other wonderful trips to Disneyland over the years with family and friends. It was no surprise then, that when my son had an opportunity to go to Disneyland on a school trip, it quickly became the most anticipated event of the year. And the best part? It would take place on his fourteenth birthday. So once again, I made sure he was prepared for the bus trip there—this time with Flaming Hot Cheetos, Cokes, Kit-Kats, a puzzle book, and of course, spending money.

Unbeknownst to me, Joe would spend his final birthday at The Happiest Place on Earth. And the year after that, Joe would spend his birthday at The Happiest Place *ever*—heaven. It wasn't a trip I was prepared for as his mom. But this I know: Joe was prepared. Not with food or drinks or crossword puzzle books. I would love to claim it was the prayers we prayed together. Or the devotions we would read at night snuggled up in his bed. Perhaps it was the many church services we went to together. The tearful conversations we had about forgiveness and love. The Christian music we sang along to in the car. The years of Christian education and learning Scripture verses.

It would be tempting to toot my own horn as a parent and claim that somehow all those things I did to nurture my son's faith played a part in him going to heaven. But it wasn't any of those things that guaranteed Joe his entrance into eternity. As much as I want the assurance and confirmation that my child is with Jesus, I only need to look at the preparation that was done *for* him, not *by* him. And not just for him, but for all of us as well.

The preparation began long before Joe—or any believer—left this world. It began in the Garden of Eden when we were promised a Savior. When God created our world, it truly was The Happiest Place, perfect in every way—that is, until sin entered the picture. And in those thousands of years until Christ came down to earth, God was preparing the hearts of His people to welcome His Son. While Jesus lived among the people, He was preparing them for His death and resurrection. When He went back into heaven, it was to prepare a place for us in His Father's mansion. But it didn't end there. Because God truly desires to be with us, He sent His Holy Spirit to prepare our hearts for the seed of faith He would plant, which He graciously does in the waters of Baptism. In those waters, we are made His children, His heirs to receive the kingdom of heaven.

As much as we'd love to take credit for the watering of our faith that grows and blossoms, the truth of it is that even those things we do—worship, prayer, devotions, service—those are all things that are *provided* by our loving God. Just as I prepared my children to enjoy their time at Disneyland, I didn't just bring them to the gate and walk away. I also provided the ticket, brought the snacks and drinks, and took them by the hand so they wouldn't get lost.

God does just the same for us. He provided the way by sending His Son to pay the price of admission into His kingdom. He gives us sustenance along the way when our feet are weary from walking. He takes us by the hand when we lose our way. And when we finally fall asleep, we rest well in His loving arms.

I can't think of a better place to spend a birthday.

PRAYER

Lord, Thank You for paying the price of admission into Your kingdom with Your blood shed on the cross. Thank you for the faith put into my heart at my baptism. Prepare my heart for the day when I, too, will get to live forever in heaven with You. Focus my eyes on what is truly important in this life to be in close relationship with You, until one day I see You face-to-face in the happiest place ever. Amen.

REFLECTION

Share your gratitude to God for paying the admission for your entrance to heaven. How can you nurture your faith as you prepare your heart for the happiest place?

_____

_____

_____

_____

_____

Letting Go

"For I am convinced that neither death nor life, neither angels nor demons, neither the present nor the future, nor any powers, neither height nor depth, nor anything else in all creation, will be able to separate us from the love of God that is in Christ Jesus our Lord."

~ Romans 8:38-39

Every time I hear the song "Let It Go" from the movie *Frozen*, I can't help but smile a little. Not because of the song itself, but because of the memories associated with it. Memories of my daughter playing it on repeat in her room at loud volumes just to annoy her brother. Hearing it on the car radio and belting it at the top of my lungs, just to drive Joe crazy. Frequently breaking into chorus at any point in the day to watch my son run out of the room screaming. Yep, I'm *that* mom.

Perhaps then, it was rather fitting that for what would have been Joe's fifteenth birthday, many family and friends gathered together at his grave to "let it go," so to speak, by releasing blue balloons with Bible verses of hope written on them. It was a moving scene to watch all those balloons drift up and be carried away by the breeze. (Well, except for the handful that flew into a nearby tree...but people need hope even at a cemetery, right?) As they floated away, I turned to see my five-year-old nephew still clutching the balloon he brought to release. It was a beautiful birthday balloon, colorful and shiny, filled with sparkly stars. I was certain he had picked it out himself.

"Let it go, buddy," my brother told him lovingly. "It's time."

My nephew looked at his dad. He looked back at the balloon. It seemed wrong to let something so special just float away. He knew he was supposed to let it go, but I could tell from those imploring eyes that he hoped he would be able to keep it. After some more gentle coaxing, though, he opened his hand and let that beautiful, shiny balloon fly away.

I smiled to myself, watching that scene. How often have *I* been holding on to what I thought was something so beautiful and perfect for me, when God was gently nudging me to let it go, to release it to His care and divine plan? And how often have I looked at what I have in my hand, then looked into my Father's eyes, doubtful that letting it go would bring about something beautiful? There have been many things I have had to let go over the years…houses, jobs, church homes, friendships—and yes, even my own son.

I know I'm not the only one who's had to "let it go." Surely, you have, too. Maybe you had to let go of a relationship you thought would last. Maybe you had to let go of a job that didn't turn out the way you thought it would. Or maybe you had to let go of the dreams you had for your future because somewhere along the line, it all got messed up. All that "letting go" might just lead us to shake our angry fists at God and remind Him of all that's been taken from us. We might feel like He doesn't fully comprehend the time or the money or the dreams we've invested into our past, present, and future, only to wind up empty-handed. How could He possibly understand?

But God *does* get it. Because *He's* had to let go, too.

From that first bite of the forbidden fruit, God knew He'd have to let go of something even more precious: His own Son. And that's just what He did. He let his only Son go down to earth to be tempted, tortured, and beaten. He let Him go to the cross to suffer and die. And when Jesus hung there, crying out to His Father, "My God, my God, why have you forsaken Me?", God did the ultimate act of letting go: He separated himself from his Son, allowing Jesus to experience hell on our behalf, so that He could get back what had originally been lost.

Us.

All of that was done so we would never have the fear of being separated from our loving Father again. Gone is the fear of sin. Gone is the fear of the devil. Gone is the fear of death. We can truly let go of all those fears. And when we do, our hands are then empty, free to reach out and grab hold of the blessings Jesus' death and resurrection gives us. Forgiveness. Grace. Eternal Life. Hope.

Our hands filled to overflowing with these gifts, we can now declare boldly to the world, just as Elsa did: the fears that once controlled me, can't get to me at all.

PRAYER

Lord, forgive me for the times I want to hang on to the things of this world and feel You owe me for what I've lost. You lost so much more when You gave up Your Son on the cross to die for me! Thank you for letting go of Jesus, so that we would never have to let go of You or the blessings You undeservedly pour out into our lives. Amen.

REFLECTION

What have you been holding on to that you could use God's help in releasing? Ask for God's help and an unshakable trust in His plan for your life.

_____

_____

_____

_____

_____

A Not-So Hollywood Ending

"Jesus said to them, 'Very truly I tell you, unless you eat the flesh of the Son of Man and drink his blood, you have no life in you. Whoever eats my flesh and drinks my blood has eternal life, and I will raise them up at the last day.'"

~ John 6:53–54

I f you ask me the question, "Have you ever seen the movie....?" there's a 90% chance, I'll answer no. It's not that I don't enjoy movies. I just don't seem to have the time or the patience to sit for more than an hour. However, despite those barriers, I finally made the commitment to watch T*he Lion, the Witch, and the Wardrobe*...about twelve years after it came out. It truly was an enjoyable movie—that is, until the epic battle scene near the end.

In case you need a little background information about said battle, allow me to recap: The evil White Witch, a.k.a. the self-proclaimed Queen of Narnia and her army stand ready to defeat the army of Aslan the lion, whom she had already killed. The Queen's army is made up of largely grotesque creatures who are poised to kill and destroy. (I'm pretty sure I'll never be able to look at yaks the same way again.) In the end, good triumphed over evil, with the resurrected Aslan coming to the rescue at just the right moment to kill the White Witch. But not before she had mercilessly stabbed the boy Edmund. That sweet boy lay on the ground, fighting for his life.

After the epic battle is finished, all of Edmund's siblings rush to his side, knowing there is nothing they can do for their dying brother. That is, until little Lucy remembers she possesses the gift of red cordial, which was given to her by Father Christmas "to heal any ailment or injury." She drops a bit of the cordial into Edmund's open mouth...and voila! Edmund is healed and whole again and hugging his rejoicing siblings in a matter of seconds. It was the perfect Hollywood ending.

Which would leave most viewers happy, satisfied, and content. But it did none of those things for me. Instead I felt angry, bitter, and jealous after turning off the television. Where was *my* perfect Hollywood ending? It wasn't there when I signed divorce papers after fifteen years of marriage. Nor was it there when I was forced to foreclose my home just a few months later. And it certainly wasn't there when my son lay on the ground, fighting for *his* life. How I wish I had had a little vial of magic red liquid to drop into Joe's mouth to save him! But there was no reunion of hugs for me on that tragic September day.

All of those difficult memories left me asking God questions. Couldn't the script have been changed? Couldn't You have decided to go a different direction with that scene? Couldn't the ending have been rewritten?

I'm sure there are things in your life that you wish could have had that perfect Hollywood ending. Or maybe you'd just settle for a different ending than how things turned out. Do you ever wonder why God didn't intervene and change the outcome? If He truly is all-powerful, then why didn't He prevent the tragedy that unfolded?

I wish I knew the answers. We've heard the many platitudes that go along with asking these questions, such as "God sees what we can't" and "we live in a sinful world" and "we aren't promised a world without pain." And while those are all true statements, we might still find ourselves having feelings of anger and injustice towards God for either not preventing the tragedies in our lives or for not changing the outcome of them.

But here is another true statement to consider when we have these questions: Satan is hard at work and wants nothing more than for us to stay angry at God. He loves when we go through trials and find ourselves distanced from God as a result. He is constantly plotting how to get us to be in his army and fight on his side. He delights in our doubts that God could still be good even when things in our life are not. He reminds us that we did not get that perfect Hollywood ending we think we deserved. With all those thoughts in our heads, we soon begin to fight a battle between what we know is the truth of God's word and the lies of the devil. Where was God when we needed Him most? Why couldn't *our* lives—or the lives of those we loved—be saved with some life-giving red liquid?

But, oh, my friends, they have indeed! Not only were our lives saved with the blood of Jesus over 2000 years ago, but we still participate in that life-giving blood every time we take communion. That liquid sustains and preserves us in faith until we see our Savior face to face and join all the saints in heaven.

Just as Aslan declared, "It is finished," when he killed the White Witch, those same words were spoken on the cross by our Savior. It meant that all 353 prophecies in Scripture were fulfilled at that moment. But here's what it comes down to for us: Sin was finished. Satan was finished. Death was finished. A life forever separated from God...also finished. That brings such an incredible peace to our hearts and sustains us on those days when everything about life seems unjust. Our trials in this world are temporary. We may not get that perfect Hollywood ending we think we deserve. But we *will* get a perfect heavenly ending we definitely didn't deserve, either.

For those of us still fighting the battle of heartache and loss, take comfort in this: we already know how the battle turns out. The enemy has been defeated. The victory of life eternal has won. And it won't be because of some Hollywood-created magic red liquid, but because of the real life-saving blood of our Lamb.

PRAYER

> Lord, it seems some days as if I am fighting a battle of many different emotions because of the struggles I am walking through. Remind me that despite my feelings of sadness or anger or disbelief, You still love me. You still fight for me. And You *did* fight for me in the epic battle against sin, death, and the power of the devil. The red liquid—Your very blood--shed on the cross gives me hope and peace and comfort in the trials of my earthly life. Thank you, Lord for winning the battle! Amen.

REFLECTION

> *What would your perfect Hollywood ending have been if you had been the director? How does knowing God has won the ultimate battle change your view of your story?*

_____

_____

_____

_____

_____

Prayer Changes Things: Part I

"Create in me a clean heart, O God, and renew a right spirit within me."

~ Psalm 51:10

For years, there has been a sign hanging in my kitchen with these three words: PRAYER CHANGES THINGS. I bought it years ago at some chain home goods store, with little thought given to the significance of the words itself. Most likely, the sign matched my decor, fit the designated space, and was affordable. It may seem odd to say, but I've had a love/hate relationship with this sign for nearly a decade. "Really?" you ask. "It's just a sign!" But trust me…there have been times I've wanted to throw this sign on the ground and stomp on it. I've wept at the sight of this sign. I've praised God for the truth of it. Before you have me committed for bipolar behavior towards a piece of wall art, let me explain.

You see, the minute (yes…the very *minute*) I learned my marriage was over, my dazed eyes just happened to wander over to those three little words hanging above my stove: PRAYER CHANGES THINGS. I stared transfixed on those words as my eyes began to well up with tears. "You've got to be kidding me about this prayer thing, right God?" I thought. "Because I'm pretty sure there is no prayer in the world that can change what's been done or fix all that has been broken." Prayer changing *anything* at that point seemed like a huge joke.

I stayed angry at that sign for a long time…well, maybe not the sign so much, but more about what it stated. Sometimes I mocked those words in disgust. Sometimes I avoided looking at them altogether, because they seemed laughable in comparison to what I was walking through. But more often than not, I started talking to God whenever I'd see them.

It wasn't anything formal that started with "Dear God" and ended with "Amen." I actually started talking *to* God. *With* God. And let me tell you, it wasn't always pretty. At times, my prayers were shouting matches with God. "How could you let this happen to me?!" They were words of disbelief and shock. "Really, God, you couldn't have let me see this coming?" Words of utter brokenness and despair. "You will *never* be able to fix my broken heart, Lord!" Words of fear about an unknown future. "How am I supposed to provide for my children now?" Those were some ugly, nasty, rebellious prayers that led me to a place of mistrust, doubt, and anger towards a loving God.

I have a feeling I am not alone in praying prayers of that nature. You may not have used those same words, but the sentiments might have been the same. When life doesn't go according to our plan, when we're blind-sighted by choices others make, or when the path we think we're going down disintegrates, we want to blame someone. Anyone. Even God. Maybe if He knew just how upset we were, He would change our circumstances. Make it all better. Fix what's been broken. Right?

Perhaps for you, that was the case. However, for me, my circumstances did not change. My life as I knew it would never go back to what it had been. Which meant something else needed to change. My angry heart. My skewed perspective. My ugly attitude. One night, as I was reading through the Psalms for comfort, I ran across one of David's prayers written thousands of years ago: "Create in me a clean heart, O God, and renew a right spirit within me." My heart was exhausted from being so full of anger and bitterness and unforgiveness. It definitely wasn't clean. And my spirit definitely wasn't right. That prayer quickly became my own. And so over the course of many days and weeks and months, I began to discover the crucial truth that was right before my eyes:

Prayer did, indeed, change things.

It didn't change the fact that I was getting a divorce. And it didn't change the fact that I had been betrayed and lied to for so many years. But what God did through my prayers (and the prayers others offered up on my behalf) was change my heart to be less angry and more loving. To be less resentful and more forgiving. He changed my attitude about what was important and what was not. He changed my relationship with Him to be a much more personal one. But most of all, prayer gave me hope that I was not alone. My husband might have walked away from our 15-year-marriage, but my heavenly Father would always be there to listen to me and to stay with me forever.

Dear one, what is it that you have been constantly praying for? Have you been relentlessly asking God to change your present circumstances? Have you been waiting for God to intercede with a particularly difficult situation? Or perhaps you have been begging God to take away the hardships of your life. He may or may not decide to do any or all of those things according to His perfect will and timing. But in the course of your conversations with Him, ask Him to not only change the *things* in your life, but to change *your heart and mind*. We can't always control the things around us—or the people. But we can always trust our loving God, who never changes, and who is always ready to listen to our prayers.

PRAYER

Lord, You are so faithful to hear my prayers and never tire of listening to me! Just as You have always listened to Your people, hear me now. Hear my cry to You for help. For comfort. For peace. For hope. Whatever needs to be changed in me, please change exactly that as You see fit. Replace the ugliness of my hurt and brokenness with Your healing and joy. Give me a heart that follows after You, Lord. Amen.

REFLECTION

Besides asking God to change your circumstances, how could you ask God to change your attitude or perspective towards that circumstance?

Prayer Changes Things: Part II

"An angel from heaven appeared to him and strengthened him."

~ Luke 22:43

O n September 6th, 2016, I walked into my house to once again be confronted by the sign that this time, hung over the kitchen sink. As I looked at those words, I didn't feel anger. Or peace. Or sadness. Or strength. I felt numb. Everything was just as the kids and I had left it nearly forty-eight hours ago. It somehow made the pain even more unbearable. Seemingly normal…and yet, nothing would ever be normal again.

My mind couldn't stop playing the horrific events that took my son's life just the day before. Prayer was an integral part of that day, but yet, here I was left to wonder, "Did prayer change anything?" I recalled the moment when I could hear my sweet friend praying the Lord's Prayer as her husband and I administered CPR. Every breath I took was a prayer. "Please save him!" I prayed with each chest compression. When the ambulance arrived, I desperately asked one of the paramedics what I could do to help. He turned to me, looked me square in the eye, and exclaimed one word:

"PRAY!"

I immediately knelt at my son's feet in the back of the ambulance and poured out the most earnest prayers I have ever prayed in my entire life. Every exhale was a prayer for my son to live. For God to be his breath. For a miracle to happen. For time to rewind just an hour. But as the minutes passed, I began to run out of words. And hope. My mind raced with thoughts of what Joe's life would become if he survived. Would he be in a coma? Would he ever be the same child I knew? Would the damage be too great? Suddenly, my prayers stopped being about what I wanted and became prayers of complete surrender to the will and sovereignty of God. He loved my son a million times more than I did. He alone knew the future. The answers. The plan.

My thoughts turned to another prayer prayed in desperation. When Jesus prayed in the Garden of Gethsemane, just hours before He knew He would suffer a horrific death, His prayer was one of utmost surrender as well.

"Father, if you are willing, take this cup from me; yet not my will,
but yours be done. An angel appeared to him and strengthened him.
And being in anguish, he prayed more earnestly,
and his sweat was like drops of blood falling to the ground."
~ Luke 22:42-44

Have you ever resonated with what Jesus was feeling, begging God for there to be a different way? Maybe it seemed like hope was running out. Like there was too much pain and sadness to continue down the path you were on. Maybe you bargained with God. If He could just do this one thing to make things turn out differently, then you would do something for Him. Anything for Him. Even if you could just hear His voice and know what to do.

Perhaps that was the case for you, but it wasn't for me. God didn't speak to me in my moment of desperate prayer. And He didn't speak to Jesus either as far as we know. You see, God's lack of answer was an answer unto itself. There was no other way. There was no changing the plan to save humanity from sin. There would be pain and sadness in the hours that followed Jesus' prayer. There would be death. It would appear as if all had been lost. The tomb would be shut. Heaven would be silent. Hope would be gone. Or so it seemed.

In the minutes after Joe died, I had a chance to sit with him in the ambulance and say my goodbyes. I thanked God for the life of my precious boy here on earth and for allowing me to be his mother. But then came the moment where the door was shut and the ambulance drove away with his body. I can still remember the eerie silence after that moment. It seemed as if all had been lost. The hope of seeing my child alive again was gone. Or so it seemed.

But I knew. I knew that wasn't the end of Joe's story.

Because it wasn't the end on that Friday over 2000 years ago.

Hope would come in the wee hours of a quiet Sunday morning. The stone would be rolled away. The grave would be empty. And death would be defeated forever.

This is what I cling to, my friends. This is what helps me put one foot in front of the other every day. Not just hope in what Jesus did, but faith that He did it. And faith that my son, as a believer in Christ, continues his story in the presence of Jesus in heaven.

While God may not have used words to respond to His Son's prayer, He did use action. He sent an angel to strengthen Jesus. And that action—that response—made all the difference in the ability of Jesus to bear the load and shoulder the way that lay before Him. By giving Jesus the strength to travel the road all the way to the cross for our sin, it did, indeed, change everything. For me. For Joe. For you. For all believers.

God didn't respond with words to my desperate prayers. He didn't change the course of what was to come and the load I'd have to bear. But He did send believers to my side and used prayer to strengthen me when I was at my weakest. I recall one of the EMT's came over to me, put his arm around me and prayed. And shortly after Joe passed away, there was a pastor and his wife waiting to sit with me and pray. To be honest, I can't remember any part of their prayers. But it wasn't the words that mattered in that moment. It was about action. It was as if God Himself was wrapping His arms around me to bring comfort to a mother who had just lost her only son.

Because He knew what it was like to lose His.

PRAYER

Lord God, there is never a moment you don't hear my desperate cries for help. Even though I desire to hear words directly from You, remind me that Your actions never fail to show me Your incredible love and strength. Thank You for giving Your Son the strength to do what needed to be done to save me. Wrap Your loving arms around me in the ways You know are best to help me bear the trials of this world, until I feel Your arms around me in the eternity of heaven. Amen.

REFLECTION

Describe a time when instead of using words, God used action to answer your prayer.

_____

_____

_____

_____

_____

Jesus Is My Pool Boy

"He gives strength to the weary and increases the power of the weak."

~ Isaiah 40:29

When people ask how we desert folks survive the intense summer heat, my response is always the same: air conditioning and a swimming pool. (I seriously have no idea how anyone survived 100+ temperatures before these things were invented.) So when I was looking for a rental home several years ago, my kids took one look at the backyard pool and diving board and knew *this* was the place we would live. And they were right.

Now, before some of you non-pool owners get any ideas about how nice it must be to just walk out the back door and jump into the cool water whenever the mood strikes, let me stop you right there. You see, not only were we fortunate enough to have a pool in our backyard, but we also were blessed with a really tall king palm tree near the pool. (Make sure to read that last sentence with a bit of sarcasm.) I mean, I know it *sounds* pretty scenic and tropical...unless you know the horrific mess that comes from having a king palm tree. If you're not familiar, just know that king palms send out these long green shoots at the end of May when the temps start heating up. And those long green shoots open up two weeks later and blossom with a bajillion little white flowers. And those little white flowers fall at the slightest of breezes. And it takes *weeks* for all of those itty bitty flowers to fall.

What does that have to do with swimming you ask? Nothing, I suppose, as long as you don't mind floating around in a pool full of little white petals, dead bees and itty bitty pieces of palm tree debris. I find the whole scenario rather disgusting, which is why I learned very quickly that at the first sight of those nasty green shoots to immediately call a landscaper to shimmy up my 30-foot palm tree and saw them off. Problem solved, right? Well, yes...except that the neighbors' king palm tree sits directly over the wall just to the southwest of my pool. And they couldn't care less about all those shoots and flowers and debris that make their way into my pool. So, therein lies the real problem: every time we want to swim, I have to spend nearly forty-five minutes skimming all the debris from a tree that isn't even *mine*. (Pity party for one, please.)

It's a back-breaking task that takes extreme patience, perseverance, and a great deal of strength, too. (And I *did* mention that it's over 100 degrees most of the summer here, right?) I can't just go out to the pool and expect to be done cleaning in a matter of minutes. I know it will be a long, arduous process. I can skim a certain area of the pool over and over and over again...just to return to the same spot and find it still a mess. Sometimes as I feel I'm nearing the end, a big gust of wind comes up to extend my cleaning time. There are moments I have to set the long pole down and take a break. My muscles ache. My back hurts. The task seems like it will never end. How I wish I had someone to take over and finish the job I can't seem to do perfectly!

In those quiet moments as I silently skim the mess from my pool, God has been speaking to my heart about this incredibly difficult journey I've been on and how much it is like this process of skimming. There is no doubt that my days are filled with so much debris and mess. Broken relationships. Loneliness. Grief. Financial worry. Anxiety. Fear of the future. The burdens of others I love. And just when I think some area of my life is "fixed" and clean, I come back to it over and over and over again, to find out what a mess it continues to be.

So many of my life's messes I did not choose. And I know you probably didn't choose yours either. How many times do you survey the mess and ask God those hard questions such as, "Why did *my* marriage have to end? Why did *my* loved one have to die? Why did *I* have to be the one to get cancer? Why do *I* have to struggle with finances? Why did this happen to *me*???" Somedays I just want to quit, don't you? I just want to put down that heavy metal skimming pole and walk away from all of life's battles.

But as much as I detest cleaning that pool and want to give up most days, I have come to two realizations. The first, and more important one, is this: It wouldn't matter if I skimmed that pool for five minutes or fifty minutes or five hundred minutes. I would never be able to fully clean up all the mess and have a perfectly clean pool to enjoy. There would always be some kind of debris floating on the surface. The same is true of life's messes. We can try to clean them up all on our own, every minute of every day, but you know what? Our lives would still be messy.

Fortunately, for us, that's where Jesus steps in. Not only did he step into our world to take on flesh, but He also stepped into a pool of water called the Jordan River—not because *He* was dirty—but because *we* were. Our sin had made a mess, not just of the world, but of ourselves. A mess so great we couldn't clean it up on our own, no matter how hard we tried. But that didn't stop Jesus from loving us. He willingly came to take that skimming pole from our hands and bind Himself to our messes through the waters of baptism, through His death, and victoriously, through His resurrection. We truly can rest from our labors, knowing that Jesus has paid it all on the cross and now redeems our messes for His purposes and His glory.

The second realization, although lesser, is still crucial. It is those very messes of life that grow a deep faith in us, strengthen us beyond anything we think we could endure, and empower us to live a life pointed to Christ. Despite my frustration over all the debris in my pool, I've developed considerable strength (and a decent tan) from those forty-five-minute upper-body workouts. If I only had a few measly leaves in my pool, my gain of strength would be quite minimal. When I stand and survey the mess before I begin, I can't help but think, "Why couldn't there just be a few leaves?" "Why couldn't the neighbor just trim his tree?" "Why is today another windy day?" But as I get to work, it hits me: The fact that so much mess blows into my pool on a daily basis, which is seemingly frustrating, is the very reason I am stronger. I have to believe that all the "junk" of my life has made me stronger as it has for you, too. And I am absolutely *certain* that it is the debris of our lives that God uses for His glory and His purposes to show not *our* strength, but *His*.

Make no mistake. There are days I don't think I have the strength to keep dragging that net around and around the pool. But as I am weary, Jesus comes alongside me with His strength as He so faithfully promises to do. And He reminds me of why I keep going, moving forward, continually skimming those itty-bitty pieces of junk. Because there is hope and *complete assurance* that when all the junk of this life is over, I'm going to put my feet into the crystal-clear waters of eternity. No skimming required.

PRAYER

Lord, I find myself so weary with all that life has thrown at me. There are days I don't think I can keep going and I want to walk away from it all. Remind me that I don't have to bear the burden of all this alone. You are there beside me, not just to encourage me, but to take the burden out of my hands and carry it Yourself, just as you carried the burden of sin all the way to the cross. I pray for Your strength to renew me as I wait for the day when all my burdens will be gone and I will rest in Your arms forever. Amen.

REFLECTION

How do you entrust life's messes to God? How has God shown that He is using those messes for His glory through you?

To Infinity...and Beyond

"When I look at the night sky and see the work of your fingers—
the moon and the stars you set in place— what are mere mortals that you
should think about them, human beings that you should care for them?"

~ Psalm 8:3–4

I recently visited Arizona State University's School of Earth and Space Exploration to watch a 3D, live-narrated program entitled "To the Edge of the Universe and Everything in Between." Unbeknownst to me, this school at ASU is a leading center for space discoveries and study. Who knew, right? Plus, the theater was overly air-conditioned, which was another determining factor to attend. (Hey, it's how we survive the brutal desert heat of summer.)

The majority of the program was to impress upon the audience the sheer vastness of space. It began by initially showing planet Earth, zoomed out to show the hundreds of satellites that revolve around our floating home, and then continued to pan out to the solar system, the exoplanets, the Milky Way galaxy, the multitude of galaxies, and beyond. Like waaaaay beyond. To something called "cosmic background radiation." What's fascinating is that new information and depth to the universe are constantly being discovered. The edge of the universe is continually being redefined. My mind was truly blown away by what the latest technology has discovered about the seemingly limitlessness of space.

But perhaps what's even *more* mind-boggling to me is that there is not one shred of information, not one piece of technology, not one single image brought to our eyes that is new to God. He knows it all. Every galaxy, every star, everything in the entire cosmos is no mystery to the One who made it all. Yet, while my mind could not even begin to comprehend the vastness of space, I began to think about how the edge of the universe is as infinite as the love of God.

Just as the show was about to wrap up, the narrator told us to sit back and enjoy as we "zoomed back in," through everything we just saw, to the planet Earth. Once again, I was awestruck...but this time not at the vastness of God, but at His intimacy. To go from the edge of forty-five billion light years away, to our rotating home of green and blue...let's just say it makes one feel pretty small in the grand scheme of things. And yet, God knows every detail of each one of us, down to our very cells.

The night before my son went to be with Jesus, I watched as he and his friend stood in an open field and stared up at the sky. In curiosity, I wandered over to them to see what they were looking at. The absolute blackness of the sky illuminated countless stars in our view—something we don't often see because of living in a large city. We commented on how vast space must be and how amazing God is to have created each star with just a word. Joe was so blown away by the sight of all those stars, he took out his cell phone in an attempt to photograph them. I was not aware at that precise moment that our friend's night vision camera recorded the final photograph I would be in with my precious boy.

But in that moment...God knew.

He knew what the next day would hold and how it would change our lives forever. It was no mystery to the Creator of the stars that one of His beloved creations was going home soon.

If you have walked the road of grief, you have most likely walked the road of guilt. You wonder what you could have said or done that would have changed the outcome. You wish there were things you would have expressed to a loved one, if you knew it was the last time you'd have an opportunity to talk to them. You say things like, "If only I had..." or "I should have...". Let me stop you right there. Do not allow the enemy to put an ounce of guilt into your heart. You are not the author of life. That job belongs to God. In the Psalm 139:16, David writes, "All the days ordained for me were written in your book before one of them came to be."

That truth is one of the hardest to come to terms with, because we'd like to think that we have control over how many days were "written" for us—or our loved ones. And yet, it is one of the most comforting lessons one who is grieving learns. To know that every day of my child's life was ordained from beginning to end, and that there was no single thing I could have done to change the course of how it ended, truly brings comfort to my overwhelmed heart on the hardest days.

My grief is constantly being redefined. But my God is not. God is who He was, who He is, and who He will be forever. The circumstances of my life do not change God's character. Nor will they ever. Instead, it is *me* who is constantly discovering the depths of His love and the infiniteness of His grace. And now I am the one who stands amazed, looking up at the heavens, blown away by what God has done and continues to do in, through, and for me.

My friend, I don't know what kind of valleys you have walked through or are walking through right now. Whether you saw it coming or you didn't, be assured that *none* of it was or is a mystery to God. His knowledge of this vast universe is certainly wise enough to know every detail of your life. His intimate love for you can fill the very depths of your broken heart as He has done for mine. His grace goes to infinity. And beyond anything we could think or imagine.

PRAYER

Lord, all You are and all You have made are so incredibly amazing! Thank You for never changing, for being the same loving, faithful God You have been since the beginning of time. Nothing is a mystery to You, including the trials I have walked through. I may not know what the future holds, but You do and that's enough. I know You are already in my future, working all things for Your good. Wrap me in Your infinite love and do immeasurably more in my life than I could ask or imagine. Amen.

REFLECTION

How does knowing that God has written all our days in His book help relieve you of any guilt you are experiencing? What comfort do you receive from knowing that God never changes?

_____

_____

_____

_____

_____

Moving Forward

"I press on toward the goal to win the prize
for which God has called me heavenward in Christ Jesus."

~ Philippians 3:14

One of my favorite childhood memories was going on our annual summer vacation. As a family of five, we couldn't afford to fly, so we'd all pile into our Pontiac 5000 sedan and travel cross-country to wherever our destination happened to be. One year, we had a particularly long drive ahead of us, so my ingenious mother wrapped up little gifts for us to open each time we entered a new state to celebrate the border crossing. My siblings and I would pour over the atlas and count down the miles until we could open our next treasure. I remember looking ahead down the seemingly endless interstate, thinking that once we crossed into a new state, the scenery would magically change. Or that perhaps there would be some large definitive boundary line surrounding the entire state to mark the difference when crossing over from one to the next. But as I soon learned, there was merely a large sign saying, "Welcome to...." And that was it. Not only was that a disappointment, but imagine my dismay when Iowa looked just like Nebraska. And eastern California looked just like western Arizona.

Funny how it's the same with years, too. We might shout, "Happy New Year!" at the stroke of midnight, only to realize that January 1 looks no different than December 31. Or we go to bed one age and wake up a year older. And yet, there is nothing that really feels any different than the night before. Nothing's changed or newly significant. (Unless you're now old enough to drive or legally drink or rent a car.

After that, there's not much to look forward to...except senior citizen discounts, I suppose.)

Knowing all that, I shouldn't have had much of an issue when I said goodbye to the age of 41, right? Was 42 really all that different? When I was 41, I had a son who would tease me mercilessly about getting older. I had a freshman in high school who was getting straight A's and had a crush on a girl. I had two children to love and care for under my roof. But 42? That age wouldn't have any of those same things. I kept wondering, "How can I turn a new age without Joe here?" I knew I didn't have a choice in the matter, but knowing that I was forced to move on to a new age while he remained forever fourteen was too much for my heart to handle. I desperately wanted time to stand still—or preferably go backwards, rather than keep marching on.

Which begs the question many of us who walk the road of grief and heartache ask: "How do I move forward from this?" Our brains seem stuck in a time when life wasn't so hard and seemingly normal. Perhaps we see our friends moving forward and celebrating twenty-fifth anniversaries, while our marriage only made it to the fifteenth. We watch as those around us take yet another family vacation, while we're just struggling to put gas in the car to make it to work. We see other children growing taller, making it to the next grade, graduating and getting married while our child rests in a grave. All around us life keeps moving forward, despite our wish for it not to.

So, what is this "pressing on" that Paul speaks about in Philippians? How did *he* keep going and moving forward despite his hardships and persecutions and grief? It was because of his focus—his goal—in the race of life. The "goal" Paul speaks about is his heavenly home and the gift of eternal life because of Jesus. He wasn't focused on earthly goals—like making it to the next birthday or anniversary or other major life achievement. To be sure, those are all wonderful blessings that God gives us on this side of eternity. But it is not those things that matter or last. While we move through this life, we keep our eyes looking heavenward towards the prize of life forever with Jesus. It is because Jesus continually moved forward toward the cross to accomplish His Father's plan on salvation for us that we will one day be the recipients of this prize. That is what we are moving forward *to* each day as we move *through* this world. It might feel as moving forward means getting further away from the time we've last seen our loved ones. But for the believer, it also means getting closer to the time when we will see them again in the presence of our Savior in heaven.

As you move through this world and your own hurts and difficulties, know that God walks with you each step of the way—at *your* pace, with loving patience and gentleness. Your earthly eyes might focus on what you think you need to be doing—or what others think you should be doing, according to a specific timeline. You don't need to move on *from* your grief, but day by day, you will move forward *through* it. And I'm learning there is a BIG difference between the two.

Today might feel a lot like yesterday. This month might have been no different than last month. Maybe this year is just as difficult as last year. But press on, my friends. Fix your eyes heavenward towards the prize. And in the words of Joe's favorite singer, Toby Mac, "Keep walking soldier. Keep movin' on. And lift your head. It ain't over yet."

PRAYER

Lord God, I sometimes struggle to move forward in my grief, especially as I see others moving on with their daily lives. Help me to let go of my expectations of what I should do and where I should be and focus solely on staying connected to You and Your Word. Give me the hope and assurance that every day on this earth brings me closer not only to those who have gone before, but more importantly, to You. Amen.

REFLECTION

How can you show yourself patience and grace as you walk through a season of struggle? Ask God to help you fix your eyes on Him, rather than on the world around you.

_____

_____

_____

_____

Worth the Wait

"For still the vision awaits its appointed time; it hastens to the end—
it will not lie. If it seems slow, wait for it; it will surely come; it will not delay."

~ Habakkuk 2:3

He was late again. I'd have to add yet another tardy to his attendance record. Surely he wouldn't miss the last day of school, would he? My answer came shortly after, when my little red-headed, freckled-nosed Kindergartner rolled in at 8:24, along with his dad, both of whom were armed with vases of flowers. One for me. One for my aide. One for the principal. After the others chose their flowers, I ended up with the vase of four pink peonies, all still tightly bound in their buds. They looked a bit scrawny in the porcelain green vase, but as the first one, and then the second and third began to open up, I was reminded of the true size of a peony. I deeply breathed in the fragrant smell and was instantly transported back to thoughts of my childhood. Sweet memories of the white peony bush in our yard in Nebraska flooded my mind and reminded me of running around the neighborhood barefoot in late spring.

I marveled at how large the flowers became after opening. To begin as the size of a small Brussel sprout and blossom into a flower nearly the size of my hand was incredible. And it was quite a fast process. I'd leave the house for a couple of hours and return to find a completely transformed blossom. So when the last flower stood alone in its vase after the others had wilted and been tossed, I had a desire to simply sit and watch it open up. I mean, surely if I sat there, I'd see *some* movement, right? So I pulled up a chair and watched that little peony. And watched. And waited. And watched some more. "Do something!" I impatiently screamed at the flower.

You know that old adage, "A watched pot never boils"? Well, the addendum to that should be, "A watched flower doesn't bloom." It was hard to wait. And tedious. And really quite ridiculous to think I'd actually see anything move. But as I watched, I began to think about my impatience with my own life and waiting a long time for it to bloom into something new. Truth be told, it's been many years of waiting to see what God is going to do with no perceived movement. I sit. I watch. I wait…and nothing. Or seemingly so. But when I looked at the complexity of all those layers upon layers of petals, I began to realize that God has slowly, deliberately, and quite carefully been peeling away the layers of what's necessary as He sees fit. I might not always be aware of all that needs to unfold, but I am trusting that God does and that He has it all worked out, according to His perfect timing.

How do I know this? Because I don't need to look any further than Scripture to know that the longest wait in history was meticulously and perfectly timed. After thousands and thousands of years, God's people finally got what they had been waiting for: a Savior. I'm sure it seemed as if the wait would never be over. Or that it wouldn't be worth the wait. But, oh, how He was! What a wonderful reminder that God always makes good on His promises and that in His perfect timing, He gives us exactly what we need. And even more, He gives us exactly *who* we need.

So many of the people I know and love are waiting for something, just as I am. And perhaps you're waiting, too. Maybe you're waiting for healing, relationships, children, retirement, new jobs, or simply vacation. And to those of you in the wait, let me share something God put on my heart as I stared at that remaining peony:

There is still beauty found in an unopened flower.

It may appear as if the bud is still shut tightly, with no sign of blossom. It may have a layer or two peeled back, with no seeming indication that more petals will open. But that doesn't mean the flower is stagnant in its growth. Or that growth will cease to happen from this point forward. Each petal unfolded is the handiwork of God, carefully thought out and timed, with *you* in mind. Celebrate each little piece of the bloom. Occasionally step back and marvel at what God has already done in your life. And trust that He will continue to work, regardless of how frustrated you get, as you continue to watch and wait.

I was reminded of that very truth on that last day of school. The tardy student of mine who brought the peonies? Every single day was tough for him. Learning didn't come easily. There were many tears, struggles, and frustrations. Most of the time he seemed tuned out as I talked or read a story. I often wondered what was going on in that sweet little head of his each day. But as I sat in front of the class, about to read the final story of the school year, this precious boy did something completely uncharacteristic. He jumped up from his spot on the carpet, ran over to me, threw his arms around me and whispered, "I'm gonna miss you." I held him tightly for just a second as my eyes filled with tears and whispered back, "Me too, buddy."

It took one hundred seventy-two days of school, but one small petal unfolded in that precious moment. And it was worth the wait.

PRAYER

Lord, I know I can be impatient with Your plans for my life when they seem to be taking too long. Forgive me for when I think I know better than You do. Give me trust to know that You are working all things for the good of those who love You. Allow my eyes to see what You have done in my life and what You are doing during my waiting. Amen.

REFLECTION

In what area of your life do you feel a sense of "impatience" with God? What might God be doing through the waiting?

_____

_____

_____

_____

_____

Steps of Grace

"The Lord makes firm the steps of the one who delights in Him;
though he may stumble, he will not fall,
for the Lord upholds him with His hand."

~ Psalm 37:23–24

I t's been a favorite pastime of my daughter's and mine to go to stores and try on crazy shoes we'd never really consider (or could afford) buying. You know the ones—four-inch spiky gold heels, strappy blue-leather wedges, furry neon pink ballet slippers. As far as we're concerned, the wilder, the better. We never actually *buy* anything—but we love to laugh at the sight of each other in shoes that are so ridiculous. We've been doing this since Ella was about five, when her little feet wouldn't even come close to fitting an adult size shoe. It didn't matter though, she'd still be in the same aisle trying on the same size shoe as me. She'd plunk her little self down on the ground to put on the shoes and hold her hand up to me to pull her up. I'd take her by the hand as we clomped down to find the closest mirror so she could see how they looked. Then she'd let go of my hand and try to walk herself, but it wasn't without some wobbles and sometimes even a fall.

One year, after we finished our annual school supply shopping trip, we decided to reward ourselves with a visit to the clearance aisles of DSW. As she grabbed a pair of multi-colored sequin heels to shove on her feet, she asked if I remembered the time she nearly twisted her ankle in a tall pair of shoes while she was running.

"Hmmm…I don't remember. When was that?" I asked.

"It was when we were picking up Joe from youth group," she casually replied.

But there was nothing casual about that comment. You see, that was only the second time in nearly a year that she had spoken her brother's name since he went to be with Jesus.

I knew that was a big step for her. But it was a reminder to me that I somehow felt I was doing this whole grief thing wrong. I had read books of advice about how to help my child navigate grief. I tried to do all the steps right, but nothing seemed to work the way it was supposed to. Which way was the right way? I felt so inadequately equipped to figure it out. There were so many times I stumbled around in my own grief, trying to walk perfectly and do all the right things, yet failing miserably. I suppose you could say it felt as unnatural and awkward as walking around in five-inch bright pink heels that were several sizes too large.

Perhaps you're not *actually* wearing an ill-fitting pair of stilettos, but maybe it feels like the "shoes" you're walking around in don't seem comfortable or familiar. Whether life threw you for a loop, or you thought you had it all together until you didn't, chances are you're trying to figure out how to get back on your feet and make it all right again. You've read the books. You've met with a counselor. You've talked with friends who maybe have gone through something similar, but you just can't help comparing how they seem to have figured it out and you're still struggling.

If you're there, let me share an important lesson that took many years to learn: there is *no* comparison when it comes to the valleys we walk in this life. None. Everyone's story is different. Every situation is different. There is no better or worse. There is no perfect way to walk through trials. It's often messy and hard and illogical and imperfect. There are wobbles and missteps and maybe even the temptation to step completely off the path God has laid out for us.

But there is someone who knows grief and hardship, yet walked a perfect road. Who took every step just the way He was supposed to. Who never once faltered in the journey. It's the same One who shows us grace upon grace when we don't do it all perfectly, despite our best efforts. Not only did Jesus take those steps all the way to the cross to redeem us, but He also steps closer to us in our daily lives to walk with us through the good, the bad, the ugly and the *really* ugly. He holds out His hand to pick us up when we fall. He steadies us as we walk. Perhaps He sends a friend to reach out to us at just the right time when we're feeling low. Or He puts a Scripture verse in front of our eyes that brings us encouragement when we need it the most. Or on days we don't feel we can go another step, He lovingly whispers to us that we are not alone and fills us with His own strength.

We may not know the next step to take in our journey, but we can know with full confidence that we don't take that step alone. We don't have to figure out how to do life perfectly, because we already have Jesus who did it perfectly for us. There might be quite a bit of stumbling, or maybe even a fall or two, but God will be there to catch us each time and firmly root us in the hope we hold on to. He is ready for you to take those steps—however big or small—into His outstretched arms.

PRAYER

Lord, when I am tempted to think I have to figure out how to walk through difficulties on my own, remind me that You are there beside me. Thank you for walking the perfect road that I could not. Just as You show me grace, help me show grace to those around me *and* myself. Be my steady hand and guide as I walk through this uncomfortable life. Amen.

REFLECTION

What is the danger in comparing your struggles to someone else's? Ask God for help in this area of your life.

_____

_____

_____

_____

_____

Surrender the Pen

"Many are the plans in a person's heart,
but it is the Lord's purpose that prevails."

~ Proverbs 19:21

One of the most rewarding yet frustrating parts of teaching Kindergarten is walking my students through the writing process. In the beginning of the year, the children simply draw pictures to tell their stories, as most of them don't have the phonetic skills to sound words out and write them down. But as the year goes on, they begin to label, write beginning sounds, stretch words out, learn and use high frequency words, and put all those things together to create sentences. By the end of the school year, my little Kinders can write several sentences about their chosen topic. It is truly a wonder to behold! But the process of getting there? Well…let's just say there are days when listening to nails scratching a chalkboard would be less painful.

The other day, one of my sweet boys sat with a blank piece of paper in front of him for the entire writing time. I checked in on him periodically to offer suggestions of stories he may want to share, but all he would quietly say was, "I just don't know what to write." I started to figure out that this little guy is a bit of a perfectionist. He didn't just want to slop anything down on the paper. He wanted it to be exactly the right thing. As the author of his story, he wanted to have purpose in his work.

We often refer to God as the author of our "story," don't we? (Although, perhaps a more accurate description is that we are merely characters in *His* story.). But God isn't sitting there with a blank piece of paper wondering how our lives should go. Unlike the uncertainty of a new writer, God already knows every detail of our lives. He is purposeful. Timely. All-knowing. He wants our lives to be a witness and blessing to others, not for our glory, but for His.

It's an interesting notion to think of your life as a story, isn't it? If you're anything like me, there are good chapters, boring chapters, exciting chapters, and sad ones, too. And then there are those chapters that you desperately wish you could just tear out of the book, because they weren't supposed to be there in the first place.

Or were they?

Perhaps this is one of the greatest dichotomies of faith to make sense of...we believe that God has written some wonderful chapters for our lives, but then we question if He really did author the completely tragic ones, too. And if so, why did He allow those chapters be a part of *our* story and not someone else's? I often find myself flipping back to the chapter called, "The Day Joe Went Home to Jesus." I don't know why the Author allowed my sweet boy's death to be written into my story. But He did. And there's no rewriting that chapter. No edits can be made. When I reread it, the outcome remains the same. As the Author, God must have seen some bigger purpose for my son's life through his death.

Which reminds us of another story. Of another Son's death. With not just a big purpose, but the *greatest* purpose. It was a purpose that was birthed from the moment sin entered the world. And it was fulfilled the second that Son— Jesus—breathed His last. It was the chapter that God knew *had* to be written, if we had any shred of hope to spend eternity with Him. And as awful as that chapter is to read or even imagine, it is the single most life-altering chapter for all humanity. I am forever indebted to the Author, because it means my son's story continues in heaven and that one day, so will mine. And so will yours in a happily forever after.

It is no mystery that God has been writing the most incredible stories since the beginning of time. Some were miraculous, like Moses' story. Some were tragic, like Job's. Some were unbelievable like

Jonah's. But they all had a different idea of what should have happened in their story. Moses didn't want to be a spokesperson to Pharaoh. Job wanted to remove the day he was born. Jonah decided to turn and run away from his calling to Ninevah. But God prevailed as the Author. And not only did He write those stories, He was the Hero, bringing great blessing out of difficult situations.

So...where are *you* in *your* story? Is your life going well and everything you dreamed it would be?

Surrender the pen to the Author.

Are you waiting for God to move in an area of your life because things aren't going according to your timetable?

Surrender the pen to the Author.

Have the trials of this world made you hopeless and weary and you aren't sure how you will make it through another day?

Surrender the pen to the Author.

I don't know how my life—or yours—will turn out. The process of letting it unfold may be painful at times. But I do know that regardless of the chapter—joyful, boring, or tragic—God will forever be the Author *and* the Hero of our stories.

PRAYER

Lord, You are the Author of my life's story. I praise You not only for the happy chapters, but ask for help in finding purpose and peace even in the ones that are difficult to read. Just as Your Son surrendered Himself to Your will and Your plan for His life, help me to do the same. Help me to let go and allow You to write my story, from beginning to end. May You be glorified in every chapter of my life. Amen.

REFLECTION

Think about the chapters in your life. Which ones would you remove if you could? How has God brought blessing even out of those difficult chapters?

Deleting the Comma

*"BUT because of his great love for us, GOD, who is rich in mercy, made us alive
with Christ even when we were dead in transgressions—
it is by grace you have been saved."*

~ Ephesians 2:4–5

My dad is the king of unusual and clever t-shirts. I'm not exactly sure when and how it all began, but as he and my mom began to travel more extensively around the world, a t-shirt was often purchased at nearly each destination they visited. Over the years, my dad's wardrobe has boasted shirts from Norway, Greece, Panama, Hong Kong, and Egypt just to name a few. But as my parents' travels have slowed down, the creativity of my dad's t-shirts has not. My sister has taken t-shirt gift giving to a new level, often scouring the internet for just the right "dad shirt" for his birthday or Father's Day. One of my all-time favorite shirts was one she purchased for him a few years ago. (It was arguably Joe's favorite as well, as it never failed to elicit a laugh from him when his grandpa wore it.) There's nothing particularly fancy about the shirt—it's a plain white tee with simplistic black lettering that reads,

"Let's eat grandpa.

Let's eat, grandpa.

Punctuation saves lives."

Now, the shirt's message is funny in and of itself, but even more so if you know my dad's affinity for precise grammar—a trait I have no doubt inherited myself.

It's interesting how one little minute stroke of the pen, such as the comma, can completely change the meaning of a sentence, isn't it? And ironically, I have been discovering the difference a comma (or rather, the *lack* of a comma) has had upon my relationship with God.

As I approached the first anniversary of my son's death, I found myself struggling. That seems like an obvious statement to make, but perhaps not for the reasons you may think. While I felt I needed to be feeling sadness and pain and reliving my loss from the year before, I was experiencing a season of joy because of a new relationship. These conflicting feelings became so burdensome to me that I brought up the issue to my counselor. I told him, "I feel like I should be more overwhelmed with sorrow at this particular point in my grief journey. But yet, I can't stop feeling gratitude and joy over what God is doing in my life. How do I reconcile having these conflicting emotions?"

After acknowledging my feelings about both issues, he said two very generic words that put everything into a new perspective. Those two words brought tears to my eyes and a better understanding of God's grace. He simply smiled and said,

"But God."

I thought a lot about those two words and how I've frequently used them over the years in my conversations with God. They've sounded something like this:

"But God, I feel so broken!"

"But God, I'm lonely!"

"But God, I'm tired of waiting!"

"But God, I didn't choose this!"

"But God, I've already lost so much!"

"But God, I won't survive this!"

Sound familiar? Maybe you have your own list of statements like I do. Every time we use a "But God, ..." phrase, that little comma sneaks right in and puts the focus on ourselves and our own personal sense of injustice in our lives. It's almost as if we're saying, "Listen, God. You don't seem to understand my plight and can't possibly know what I'm walking through, so let me lay it out for You." As if God doesn't see or know our hearts better than we do.

So when my counselor said those two words, "But God," it took me a second to realize there was no comma after it. And when there was no comma, I began to figure out that the phrase "But God" had nothing to do with me at all. Instead, it had everything to do with God's character and His action *toward* me.

I decided to scour Scriptures that used the "But God..." phrase and to my amazement, found more than 30 examples of those two words side by side that clearly describe who God is and what He's done. Take a peek:

*"...**but God** intended it for good to accomplish what is now being done, the saving of many lives."*
~ Genesis 50:20

*"...**but God** has surely listened and heard my prayer."*
~ Psalm 66:19

*"...**but God** is the strength of my heart and my portion forever."*
~ Psalm 73:26

*"**But God** raised him from the dead."*
~ Acts 2:24

*"**But God** has helped me to this very day."*
~ Acts 26:22

*"**But God** demonstrates His own love for us in this..."*
~ Romans 5:8

*"**But God** had mercy on him...to spare me sorrow upon sorrow."*
~ Philippians 2:27

*"**But (that) God** loved us and sent His son as an atoning sacrifice for our sins."*
~ 1 John 4:10

Did you notice that *none* of those passages contained a single comma after the name of God? Because the comma's purpose is to separate. And when we continually interject the comma, we begin to separate ourselves from what God is doing and lose trust in His plan for our lives. But when we *delete* the comma, the focus is no longer on ourselves. In grammatical terms, *God* is the subject and the rest of the sentence becomes the predicate. If you look up the verses before the above references, you'll notice that preceding the words "but God" not only contain a comma, but all point to the failings of the world and the people in it—us. In short, we mess up, but God redeems. God becomes the focus and who He is and what He has done is what remains. He listens. He helps. He demonstrates. He has mercy. He loves. He sent. He raised.

Oh, and how that last action made all the difference for us as believers! Paul reminds us in Ephesians 2, that despite our sinfulness, grace was shown. Not because of anything we did, but because of the love and mercy of our Father. It is that very love, mercy, and grace, that even on those difficult anniversaries, we can cling to more than anything. It is why there can be joy in the midst of sorrow. Peace in the midst of sadness. Hope in the midst of despair. And happiness in new beginnings, even while acknowledging the pain of the past.

PRAYER

Lord, forgive me when I make my cries to You all about me and the injustices I've endured. In those moments, bring to my mind the greatest injustice of all—that Your Son endured the cross to pay for my sins. And in doing so, His actions ended our separation from You forever. Thank you that Your love for us is never ending. And that You can bring joy, peace, and hope from the ashes. Amen.

REFLECTION

Which "but God" phrase do you use when life seems unfair? Which "but God" phrase from Scripture brings you the most encouragement on hard days?

When It's Not Always Well

And Lord, haste the day when my faith shall be sight,
The clouds be rolled back as a scroll;
The trump shall resound, and the Lord shall descend,
Even so, it is well with my soul.

~ Horatio Spafford

In 1873 Horatio Spafford put his wife and four daughters aboard a ship traveling from the United States to Europe, with the intention of following them a few days later for a family vacation. The Spaffords had already suffered the death of their young son and lost all of their properties in the Chicago Fires. A trip to get away was definitely in order. However, the ship Mrs. Safford and her girls were sailing on collided with another ship while en route, causing the boat to sink. The vast majority of the 313 passengers drowned in the ice-cold waters of the Atlantic. While Horatio's wife was rescued after being found clinging to part of the ship's debris, his daughters did not survive. Spafford left on the next ship to be with his wife after learning the tragic news. As his ship passed by the exact spot where his daughters died, he penned the words to the beloved hymn, "It Is Well." The words of this grieving father have been an inspiration to me in light of such personal loss, as I'm sure they have been for many. If one can say "It is well" when reeling from the death of not one, but *five* children… wouldn't we all consider that to be a person of great faith?

At one point, I would have agreed with that. And many a time, I have sat at my piano and sung those same words, thinking that I, too, must be a person of great faith to even be able to utter such lyrics. After all, wasn't it a great demonstration of my unshakable trust in God to accept and be okay with "my lot" in life? If I wasn't able to sing those words, it seemed to be a denial of that very faith I claimed to have.

But as time continued to pass in my grief journey, I found it more and more difficult to sing, let alone, *hear* those familiar words:

> *When peace, like a river, attendeth my way,*
> *when sorrows like sea billows roll;*
> *whatever my lot, Thou hast taught me to say,*
> *"It is well, it is well with my soul."*

If I'm being completely honest, losing my son is *not* well with my soul. And I have come to the conclusion that on this side of heaven, it never will be.

It is not well with me that Joe didn't get to graduate from high school.

It is not well with me that other kids his age got to experience homecoming and prom.

It is not well with me that he never learned to drive a car.

It is not well with me that I go to our favorite sushi restaurant without him.

It is not well with me every time I take out two plates for dinner, rather than three.

It is not well with me that his room remains empty day in and day out.

I am learning that as long as I have breath in these earthly lungs, my heart and my mind will never be "well" with Joe's death. There will never be a day where I don't long to see his face and wrap my arms around him. And that is perhaps one of the most important lessons I've learned in grief:

It's OK to not be OK.

There are other things that are not okay with me. And I'm sure it's no different for you, too. Perhaps we're not well with a diagnosis we've received. Or with a job we've lost. Or with the ending of a relationship. Maybe we turn on the TV and are not well when we see the difficulties of the world around us. When we look at the devastation of hurricanes and earthquakes and fires and violence, it is not well with our mind. When we see those around us suffering with illness and cancer and Alzheimer's, it is not well with our heart. When we hear about death of any kind, our hearts are broken for those who now have to walk their own difficult journey. It's not well with us. At all.

If all of this is not well with us, it begs the question....what *can* we be well with? More specifically, what can *our souls* be well with?

Our souls can be well with the sovereignty of God.

We can be okay knowing that God is God and we are not. God is in control of all things He created. He owns all things, knows all things, rules all things. Nothing that happens in our lives is a mystery to Him. Even the death of those we love.

"Remember the former things, those of long ago; I am God, and there is no other; I am God, and there is none like me. I make known the end from the beginning, from ancient times, what is still to come. I say, 'My purpose will stand, and I will do all that I please.'"
~ Isaiah 46:9–10

Our souls can be well with God's plan for our lives.

We can fully trust that God has a plan with a much bigger perspective than we will ever know or understand. He sees the big picture and, ultimately, it is not about *God* living out His part in *our* story. Rather, it is about us living out our part in *His* story.

"Many are the plans in a person's heart, but it is the Lord's purpose that prevails."
~ Proverbs 19:21

Our souls can be well with God's mercy.

There is never a greater awareness of the mercy of God than when walking through the journey of grief. It is because of this undeserved mercy that I have the assurance of seeing my son again. My child was saved because of the mercy of God through Jesus Christ. One day I will be too. And so will you. And this is what will ultimately reunite us in a life that never ends!

"In His great mercy He has given us new birth into a living hope through the resurrection of Jesus Christ from the dead, and into an inheritance that can never perish, spoil or fade. This inheritance is kept in heaven for you..."
~ 1 Peter 1:3–4

And finally, our souls can be well with Christ's return like never before.

Joe and I used to reference that often. Whenever we were dealing with difficult issues or would watch depressing news stories, one of us would turn to the other and say, "Time for Jesus to come back." And the other would agree. But let me tell you, a grieving mother's heart could not mean it any more sincerely to say those same words and pray it to come true every day.

"For the Lord Himself will descend from heaven with a cry of command, with the voice of an archangel, and with the sound of the trumpet of God. And the dead in Christ will rise first."
~ 1 Thessalonians 4:16

One of the final verses Horatio Spafford wrote is no mystery to those of us who long for Christ's return with every fiber of our being.

> But, Lord, 'tis for Thee, for Thy coming we wait,
> The sky, not the grave, is our goal;
> Oh, trump of the angel! Oh, voice of the Lord!
> Blessed hope, blessed rest of my soul!

God knew we would have to walk through trials in this life. He knew the moment sin entered the world that it would not be well with His soul or ours. Which is why He sent His only Son to die the death we deserved. So that there would be no more separation. No more sadness. No more grief. No more death. He made a way so that it would truly be well between Him and us. Forever.

And that is why we can declare this truth truly *is* well with our soul.

PRAYER

> Lord, there are so many things about this life that I simply
> don't feel well with. But I know that's because this world is
> not my home. The things that my soul is well with are who
> You are and what You've done in my life. I know my sadness
> will come to an end, because You have promised it would. I
> know one day all will truly be well in the presence of heaven.
> Thank you for that assurance, Lord! Amen.

REFLECTION

What is your soul "well with" when it comes to who God is and
what He's doing in your life?

_____

_____

_____

_____

_____

What I Didn't Deserve

"For all have sinned and fall short of the glory of God, and all are justified
freely by his grace through the redemption that came by Christ Jesus."

~ Ephesians 3:23–24

In 1971, McDonald's came out with one of the most successful advertising jingles in commercial history. If you're from my generation (Gen X or earlier), you'll certainly remember it: "You deserve a break today, so get out and get away to McDonald's..." The concept of "deserving a break" at Micky D's continued throughout the 70's and most of the 80's. McDonald's wasn't the only company to get consumers to feel they were deserving of some better product or idea. From diet fads claiming to give you the "body you deserve" to self-help books promising to give you the wealthy, happy future you deserve, we consumers started to believe that we were actually *entitled* to these things. Even political candidates declare in their ads that, "We *deserve* better!" than what we're currently experiencing.

Not only does the outside world feed us the belief we are somehow more deserving of greatness, but we do the same thing in our own minds, don't we? Maybe we've had a rough day at work and we feel we deserve that glass of wine. Or we've completed a hard workout and we tell ourselves we deserve that In-N-Out burger and fries. (I may or may not be speaking from personal experience here.) Maybe our kids are driving us nuts and we deserve a night out or that weekend getaway. And slowly, we begin to think that enduring tough circumstances in life, whether great or small, earns us something better, something we believe we need.

Or maybe we think that doing something good means we deserve something good in return. We work hard at our job and we deserve that raise. We've lost a few pounds and deserve a new outfit. We've poured time and energy into a relationship and we deserve the same in return. We've done our best to raise healthy, happy children and we deserve their love, respect, and obedience. Right?

After several years of walking through some pretty deep valleys, I experienced a season of joy and newness. People began to comment, "I'm so happy for you! You deserve it!" or "If there's anyone who deserves this, it's you!" While a small part of me was tempted to respond with, "I know, right?," the majority of me was wondering why I was considered to be deserving of such happiness in someone else's eyes. Did walking through brutally difficult circumstances in life *earn* me this happiness?

Let me say this with 100% assurance: Not. One. Little. Bit.

You see, I've concluded that there are two veins of thought to be had on this topic of "deservedness," and it all comes down to whether we believe *we* are in control of our lives or if we believe *God* is in control.

When we believe *we* are in control, our thinking may sound something like this: "I did this good thing; therefore, I deserve something good in return." Or "I don't deserve this bad thing because of the good I've done." Either way, both avenues of thought breed a sense of entitlement. And friends, I have been there too many times. Shouting at God that I did not deserve what had happened to me. And if you're being honest, you probably have too. It's the age-old question we are constantly trying to answer of "Why do bad things happen to good people?"

I don't think any of us would say that there aren't bad things in this life. But what about the second half of that question? How are we defining "good"? If we're nice to others? Give generously? Show patience? I hate to break it to you, but there actually is no "good" person on this planet. Not me, not you, not Mother Teresa, the Pope, or anyone else who has ever walked this earth or who ever will.

Whether you sin one time a day or a thousand times a day, it doesn't matter.

> *"No one is righteous—not even one....No one does good, not a single one."*
> ~ Romans 3:10, 12

And we *all* fall short of the glory of God. There is nothing "deserving" about us. We have earned *no good thing* in this life.

> *"He repays everyone for what they have done;*
> *He brings on them what their conduct DESERVES."*
> ~ Job 34:11

You and I deserve nothing. Well...almost nothing. Because we all sin and fall short, we do deserve *some*thing: eternal death and separation from God. But here's the crazy part.

> *"He does not treat us as our sins DESERVE or repay us*
> *according to our iniquities."*
> ~ Psalm 103:10

Can you even believe it? We deserve death, but God treats us as if we don't. That's a game-changer for our lives! What's even more unbelievable is that the only person who *didn't* deserve death is the sinless One who died for us. Even Pilate said during Jesus' trial, "He has done nothing to deserve death" (Luke 23:15). The criminal who hung on the cross with Jesus also recognized this. "We are punished justly, for we are getting what our deeds deserve. But this man has done nothing wrong" (v. 41). But perhaps Timothy puts it best:

> *"Here is a trustworthy saying that DESERVES full acceptance:*
> *Christ Jesus came into the world to save sinners—of whom I am the worst.*
> *But for that very reason I was shown mercy so that in me, the worst of sinners,*
> *Christ Jesus might display His immense patience as an example*
> *for those who would believe in Him and receive eternal life."*
> ~ 1 Timothy 1:15–16

When we begin to understand that *God* is ultimately the one in control, and has been since the beginning of time, we realize that the word "deserving" has no part in what has happened in our life, good *or* bad. The "bad things" are a result of living in a sinful world. And the "good things" are a simply a result of having a loving, merciful God. We start to realize that God is the same yesterday, today, and forever—independent of our positive and negative circumstances. He already gave us what we didn't deserve—eternal life— because of who He *is*. Not because of who we are or what we've done. But because of what His son did for *us*.

As I stood at my fourteen-year-old son's grave yesterday, those little twinges of, "I don't deserve to be standing here" came creeping up again, ready to give way to a full-blown pity party. But as I read Joe's favorite verse engraved on his marker, as I have done so many times, my eyes were opened to an amazing undeservedness of God's love.

> *"How great is the (undeserved) love the Father has lavished on us,*
> *that we should (undeservedly) be called children of God.*
> *And (even though we didn't deserve it) that is what we are!"*
> ~ 1 John 3:1

Ok, so maybe I added a few extra words that weren't there. But it turned my near pity party into feelings of incredible gratitude for what Christ did for me. For my son. And for each one of us who believes in the undeserved love of God.

PRAYER

Lord, I am so undeserving of the many gifts you've given me, but mostly the gifts of Your forgiveness, grace, and salvation. Thank You for sending Jesus to endure the death I surely deserved. When I begin to feel entitled, help me recognize that You are the same loving God, despite the good or bad circumstances in my life. Every good gift comes from You! Amen.

REFLECTION

Are there things in life you feel you deserved that you didn't get, or
that you got and didn't deserve? What has God given you that you
didn't deserve?

A Mary Christmas to You

"But Mary treasured up all these things and pondered them in her heart."

~ Luke 2:19

One of the best parts of teaching first grade was introducing the kids to chapter books read aloud. A favorite series of ours were the mysteries of Cam Jansen, the fifth-grade girl detective. Cam, short for "Camera" had a photographic memory and would often use the pictures she had taken in her mind to solve whatever mystery was at hand. Several times throughout the story, Cam would happen upon a scene, close her eyes and say, "Click!" And the image would stay in her mind until she needed to retrieve it.

Whether or not you claim to have a photographic memory, chances are you can go back in your mind to any significant life event and remember some memory, some scene, some feeling about that moment. A surprise birthday party...click! A fun family vacation... click! Graduation...click! Your wedding day...click! Having a child... click! But life isn't just a series of fun and exciting events. Even the difficult memories get recorded in our minds, too. A cancer diagnosis....click. A spouse walking out the door...click. A rebellious child breaking the rules yet again...click. The loss of someone you love... click. Unfortunately, we don't get to always choose the things our mind remembers.

Since my son passed away last year, my memory has taken a significant beating. I thought perhaps it was just my own experience, but it actually is a proven scientific fact that memory impairment is a result of grief (sometimes referred to as "grief brain"). Many others who walk the road of loss would attest to this as well. A year after losing Joe, my brain slowly began to handle and process information better than it had been. After so many months spent in a perpetual fog, I started to act like Cam Jansen, consciously and deliberately trying hard to remember events and moments as they happened.

So perhaps it was no surprise that when Christmas rolled around, I found myself drawn to one particular verse from the account of Luke 2.

"But Mary treasured up all these things and pondered them in her heart."

Mary didn't have a selective memory. Scripture says she "treasured up *all* these things..." The good. The bad. And most certainly, the incredibly difficult. And not only did she remember it. She *treasured* it. Mary, despite her circumstances, takes it all in and counts it as a treasure. A gift. Which makes sense, because a baby being born is a miraculous event, right? But what about that Friday when she watched her son be mocked, whipped, and nailed to a cross? How about when Jesus hung there and was thirsty and bleeding—and there was nothing she could do to make it all better? Did she "treasure up" those memories, too? Perhaps not in the same way she did His birth, but there is no doubt Mary had images she wouldn't be able to get out of her mind, no matter how hard she tried. She would spend that day and the next pondering. Contemplating how this had happened. Wondering if there could have been a different way. Meditating on the new reality of her life.

But God took that tragic event in history and redeemed it for His ultimate purpose—the salvation of our souls. We can look back on that moment and know how it happened. Our sin put Him there. We can wonder if there could have been a different way, but this was the *only* way. And the new reality for our life? Wonderful. Glorious. Redeemed. Saved.

And so my encouragement to you this season is not only to have a Mary kind of Christmas, but a Mary kind of life. The kind where your mind and heart stops at the wonderful, the simple, and the not-so-easy and pauses to say, "click," without your iPhone in hand. To treasure those moments, to keep them in your heart, and to count each one as a gift. *Because God redeems even the difficult moments.*

My mental photo album this Christmas had some good shots. Singing "Silent Night" by candlelight in church next to my beautiful daughter...click! Taking in the awe-inspiring colors of a sunset hike on Christmas Day...click! And it had some bad shots, too. Only filling one child's stocking...click. Sitting at my son's grave with a poinsettia in hand...click. But even those imperfect pictures remind me that although life can be terribly hard some days, it can also be full of joy. They remind me of how precious everyday life is. They remind me there is so much more beyond this earthly life and its temporary joys and sadness. But most of all, they remind me there is hope of a future with God forever, because of the gift that He gave at Christmas in His own Son, Jesus.

Immanuel has come to be with me in all my difficult pictures. And He's come to be in yours, too. May *you* have a Mary kind of Christmas, treasuring the perfect gift of Jesus.

PRAYER

Lord, the holidays can be so hard on my heart. Help my mind as it remembers the good and celebrates You and all You've given me. But help me to remember the difficult things, too, so I can be reminded of how necessary it was for You to send Jesus to be my Savior. Without Your son, there would be no hope of eternal joy. You are my greatest treasure, Lord! Amen.

REFLECTION

Share some of the good AND more difficult holiday pictures you have mentally taken. Ask God to show you ways He has blessed you even in those harder moments.

Butterfly Skin

"The Word became flesh and made His dwelling among us..."

~ John 1:14

A few years ago, I was introduced to a little Kindergartner down the hall from my classroom who was born with a genetic skin condition called epidermolysis bullosa, also known as "Butterfly Skin." I didn't know anything about EB, nor had I even heard of this rare connective tissue disorder. But one look at this sweet girl is all it took to see that her appearance was markedly different than any other child's skin I had ever encountered. Her paper-thin skin was dotted with blisters, sores, and small tears. In all other aspects, she was a perfectly normal child, but we as a teaching team knew we would have to educate our students on why this little girl's skin looked completely different from theirs.

I'll never forget how her mother calmly and patiently sat in front of my class with several sheets of tissue paper to show them why her daughter's skin was so fragile. She explained that for most children, there are several layers of skin to protect the bones and muscles underneath. One child came up to try to rip all those layers at the same time and struggled to do so. Then she laid just one piece of tissue paper over her arm. "But this is how *her* skin is," she said, referring to her daughter. My students' eyes widened as they realized just how easy it would be to rip through only that one piece of tissue. "You might bump the edge of a table or chair and it's no big deal," she continued. "But when a child with EB does that, it's a very big deal. It will cause a huge bump or blister that will take a long time to heal. It's like her skin is as fragile as a butterfly's wings." The children's heads nodded in understanding.

Over the years, I've seen this brave girl limp around campus with blisters on her feet. I've watched as her friends pushed her in a wheelchair when walking was too difficult. I've observed her hands wrapped in gauze more times than I can count. And despite the smile on her face, my heart can't help but break a little each time, knowing that she simply can't live life as a normal little girl.

As I finished the "year of firsts" without my son, I realized that my grief wasn't so much about surviving each day, but processing the reality of what happened and coming to a place of acceptance about it. And that was a very difficult place to be. Emotions constantly seemed to be close to the surface and one slight little trigger…or bump…may just cause a huge wound to open up that will take a long time to heal. Some days I'm walking and some I'm limping. And I know that I can't live life as a "normal" mom anymore.

It's as if my fragile heart has developed butterfly skin.

We often think that walking through trials and tragedies in life makes us stronger. We admire those people who seem to have a "thick skin," where nothing appears to bother them. We're encouraged as children to "be tough" when we get hurt. But truth be told, dealing with loss and pain and the difficult things of this world only end up peeling off layer after layer of our emotional skin.

God knew this would be this case for His creation, even though it wasn't as He intended it to be. He watched for thousands of years as His people walked though suffering, pain, and loss. He saw their skin getting thinner and thinner. And then He did what He had promised. He sent Himself with skin on. He sent Jesus.

And not only did Jesus live and dwell among us, but He taught. He listened. He healed. And then He did the unimaginable. He willingly chose for His skin to be beaten, whipped, torn, nailed, and pierced.

For me. For you. And for all of His Father's creation. Because ultimately...He loved.

"But He was pierced for our transgressions, He was crushed for our iniquities;
the punishment that brought us peace was on Him,
and by His wounds we are healed."

~ Isaiah 53:5

Healed. And not only healed, but *saved.* Like a butterfly emerges from its chrysalis, Jesus emerged from the tomb after three days, with a beautiful new skin to prove once and for all that He overcame death forever.

What about you, dear one? What bumps and bruises have you gotten along the way? Is your skin thin and vulnerable from all you've walked through? Do you wish that life's circumstances wouldn't have impacted you as much as they have and you had thicker skin to handle the blows?

As much as we may hope and pray for this, the ultimate healing of our "butterfly skin" won't come until we're in the presence of Jesus. But while we wait for that day, we can choose to see our fragile skin as a gift. Not because of the circumstances of how it came to be, but because of how God is using it to shape who He wants us to be. Yes, our emotions may just be under the surface, but God uses that very thing to help us feel more deeply for others in their pain.

"Praise be to the God and Father of our Lord Jesus Christ, the Father of
compassion and the God of all comfort, who comforts us in all our troubles,
so that we can comfort those in any trouble with the comfort
we ourselves receive from God."

~ 2 Corinthians 1:3–4

God is our ultimate healer and comforter. But we also know He has used many people to bring that healing and comfort to our hearts. Perhaps one day, God will use us and what we have walked through to help others receive that same comfort. What a wonderful gift it will be when God calls us to be "Jesus with skin on" to those around us!

PRAYER

Lord, You know how fragile my heart is each day. But You also know just how to heal it with Your gentleness, patience, and love. May I extend those same qualities to those around me whose hearts are hurting and are in need of healing. I praise you for the gift of sending Your Son to willingly bear the scars on His skin to pay for our sins and our ultimate healing in heaven. Amen.

REFLECTION

How would you describe the "thickness" of your emotional skin?
How can your fragile skin be used as a gift to bring comfort to others?

_____

_____

_____

_____

_____

The Cone of Shame

"Jesus cried out in a loud voice, 'Eli, Eli, lema sabachthani?'
(which means 'My God, my God, why have you forsaken me?')"

~ Matthew 27:46

The cone of shame. Pet owners—you know it well. Perhaps it was from a surgery, an infection, or a wound of some kind that warranted your pet to wear one of these unsightly contraptions. They're not only a pain for the animal, who now struggles with attempting to judge distances as they eat, drink, and navigate the corners of their surroundings, but they're also a pain for the owner as well. Quite literally. We recently were in the "cone of shame" days at our house, and I can't tell you how many times the back of my legs got scraped by the cone as my dog kept following me just a *little* too closely. But I'll gladly take the scrapes, knowing that things could have been much different.

The cone-wearing was the result of a seemingly innocent walk around the neighborhood. However, it quickly turned into a nightmare as another dog broke loose from a twelve-year-old boy's grip while my little dog and I were within just mere feet of passing. I had no time to react and pull Biscuit to safety in my arms. My seventeen-pound Chihuahua mix was no match for the gray and white Pitbull that came at him. I tried to snatch up my baby while he was still on his leash, which only succeeded in ejecting his flailing body from the harness. Being unable to grab him, I watched helplessly as the large dog tore into him, shaking him in his mouth, drops of bloods splattering the ground. The following minutes were a blur. I remember screaming hysterically. I remember trying to kick the dog and hit him with the leash. I remember the adult owners coming outside to try to get their dog off of mine. It was a feeling of complete helplessness.

A feeling I knew all too well. A trauma I knew all too well. But after the owners had finally secured their attacking dog, I snatched Biscuit up and wrapped him in my arms, blood and all, and held him close. What else would I have done? Left him there for dead? Turned my back on him and walked away when he needed his mama to rescue him? Of course not!

And yet, as I sat in church, just days later on Good Friday, hearing the crucifixion story for what seemed like the hundredth time, it hit me. That's *exactly* what God did to His Son.

Let that sink in for a moment. Jesus had endured a most brutal attack on His innocent body. Blood was shed. And in those final moments as He hung on the cross, when He was helpless and left to die, His Father turned His back. Walked away. Abandoned His own Son. By doing so, Jesus experienced the full punishment of sin on our behalf. Perhaps we try to imagine what that would have been like to be there and witness Jesus' death. Or maybe we've even tried to imagine what it would have felt like to suffer as Jesus did. But have we ever imagined that Friday from the perspective of the Father? Have we truly considered what the *Father* endured for us? How *He* must have felt as He watched his only Son be brutally beaten, mocked, spat upon, tortured, crucified?

But the truth is, He wasn't watching *helplessly*. He was watching *willingly*. Because His will was to sacrifice His Son. It was His will for Jesus to take on that cone of shame—*our* shame—and carry it all the way to the cross, humiliated and exposed on our behalf. It was the only way to ensure our forgiveness, salvation, and a life forever with Him. Without separation. And that kind of unfathomable, overwhelming, unexplainable love...it leaves me speechless.

Friends, that kind of love didn't end the day Jesus died. It is a love that has been in existence from the beginning of time. It is a love that has never failed us for a second of our lives. It is a love that constantly pursues us day in and day out. It is a love that will never end and never fail. It is a love that loves us in our darkest moments, our deepest sins, and our greatest victories.

Easter is indeed a victory for us. Not because of anything we have achieved, but because it is the ultimate celebration of God's love for us. Our cone of shame is no longer. Jesus bore it, God removed it, and we are now free. We undeservedly get to share in the victory of life after death. Instead of leaving us speechless, God's love causes us to cry out with a shout of thankfulness, "Alleluia! He is Risen!"

Shortly after hearing the crucifixion story on that Good Friday, I joined with those around me in a familiar hymn:

> *How deep the Father's love for us,*
> *How vast beyond all measure,*
> *That He should give His only Son*
> *To make a wretch His treasure.*
> *How great the pain of searing loss–*
> *The Father turns His face away,*
> *As wounds which mar the Chosen One*
> *Bring many sons to glory.*

Those very wounds brought *my* son to glory. And they will bring us to glory as well. One day, we will trade our cone of shame for a crown of victory, where we will be with our Savior forever.

PRAYER

Lord, there are so many things that overwhelm me about the truth of Your Son's death and resurrection. But knowing that You chose to walk away from Your Son in His greatest hour of need—because You wanted me to be with You forever—is a love like nothing I've ever known. Thank You for the undeserved gift of that love and for all the gifts Your Son won for us on the cross. Amen.

REFLECTION

What part of the Good Friday story impacts you most and why?

_____

_____

_____

_____

My Waze vs. God's Waze

"'For My thoughts are not your thoughts, neither are your ways My ways,'
declares the Lord. 'As the heavens are higher than the earth, so are My ways
higher than your ways and My thoughts than your thoughts.'"

~ Isaiah 55:8–9

Every morning at approximately 7:05 a.m., I open up my trusty traffic app Waze. If you're not familiar with Waze, it's an app similar to Google Maps, in which it shows you the fastest possible route to get to where you need to go. It also displays alternate routes, the time it will take to get there, HOV lane times, accidents, road hazards, and police sightings. Traffic apps are a near-necessity if you live in a large city with freeways and need to get to work on time each day. Each day I'm faced with the decision of how I should get to work. Do I chance it on Highway 51, which is usually the fastest route? Do I take the scenic backway down Tatum Road, which is now under construction? Or do I start on the freeway and bail halfway through? Making the wrong choice means I could be sitting in a huge traffic jam and be late to work. This is why I rely on Waze to tell me what to do, where to go, and how to get there. (Plus, that way if I am late, I can always blame it on the app.) But regardless of which route I take, one thing is certain: I will arrive at my desired destination.

There are many times I've wished there was a Waze app for life. Deciding on a college, a career, a spouse, a home…just click and show me my options, okay, God? Then I'll pick the one that works best for me. But life doesn't work that way, as we've well discovered. We've all dealt with those "what-ifs" in life. Perhaps even more so when we go through difficulties. When our job demands a lot from us and we feel burned out, we wonder if we chose the right career. When things start to break down and need fixing, we wonder if we made the right choice of home or car. When our marriage struggles or falls apart, we wonder if we should have never walked down the aisle. And the list of second-guessing ourselves goes on.

On what would have been my son's 16th birthday, I went to the grocery store, picked up some sushi for dinner, found a lovely arrangement of blue flowers, and selected a colorful "Happy Birthday" balloon. Then I drove to the cemetery. As I sat at Joe's grave, those "what-if" thoughts began to creep in and I wondered how I could have changed the outcome of this awful 16th birthday. What if we had stayed home that Labor Day weekend? Or just left an hour earlier? What if we had played one more game of UNO at the cabin? What if I had just said something differently to him moments before the accident? I replay the scene over and over again in my head about what I could have done differently that would have altered the course of the tragic event that took my son's life.

Do you ever play that "what if" game in your head, too? Do you wish you could go back and rewind time to do something differently, so that you don't find yourself in your current circumstances? I've been there more times than I can count. Which is why I find the scripture from Isaiah 55 comforting. Because when it comes down to it, do I want *my* way? Or do I want *God's* way? That can be a tough question to answer, because we want God's way to be *our* way. But that isn't always the case, is it? Maybe if we just had an explanation from God about why things turned out a certain way, we'd be more understanding. Perhaps like me, you are still waiting on that explanation. We might get it. We might not. But faith says it doesn't matter. It doesn't rely on explanations. It relies on the sovereignty of God to accomplish His purposes.

The will of God is not one of multiplicity. It is singularly focused: that all would come to know Him as the only means of salvation, so that we could spend eternity with Him. He may accomplish that will in a myriad of ways. It might be the way we would choose. And it might not be.

But God's ways are higher than our ways.

We may not understand why a loved one didn't get to experience a full life and was seemingly taken too early.

But God's ways are higher than our ways.

We may not understand why God isn't opening doors and moving mountains for something we've been desperately praying about for a long time.

But God's ways are higher than our ways.

We may wrestle with the fact that people we dearly love are walking through deep dark valleys with no end in sight.

But God's ways are higher than our ways.

We may not have the ability to understand God's ways. Nor might we agree with them. While our limited thoughts often focus on earthly happiness and comfort, God sees the bigger picture of preparing us for an eternity with Him. Therefore, we can surrender each thought, each struggle, each worry, and each heartache to a sovereign God, who sees far beyond our limited view of life. It requires trust and faith and dependence…all of which we never seem to have enough. Yet, God is still faithful and gracious enough to provide even those very things we lack. Because He Himself is enough. And He promises He will do what He desires to accomplish His will.

So today, and tomorrow, and every day after, let's remind ourselves over and over and over that our ways are not God's ways. And as it turns out, that's a very good thing. As much as we will never understand why we go through earthly struggles, let us be even more baffled by God's love and grace in our lives. To sacrifice a Son? That wouldn't have been our way at all. Not in a million years. But praise be to God that His way was not ours. His way atoned for our sins and guaranteed the destination of heaven with Him. A destination which the saints who have gone before have already reached. A destination filled with joy and peace—and undoubtedly no traffic jams.

PRAYER

> Lord, I may not always understand the path life has put me on or why I've had to endure difficult trials. In those moments where I question You and become frustrated with my circumstances, give me a deep faith and trust to be at peace, knowing that Your ways are higher than mine. You see everything from a heavenly perspective and have a desire for everyone to be in a saving relationship with You. Help me keep my eyes fixed on the destination of eternity with You. Amen.

REFLECTION

Describe a "what if" scenario you often play in your head.
What comfort does it bring knowing that your ways are not God's ways?

_____

_____

_____

_____

_____

Shared Custody

"So, whether we live or die, we belong to the Lord."

~ Romans 14:8b

It doesn't seem so long ago that I used to relish trips to Target and wander the aisles, just so I could have a "break" from being a parent for an extra thirty minutes. I can remember the anticipation of a babysitter arriving, which meant having *multiple* hours away from my needy kids, even if it meant shelling out some extra cash. And then there were those special getaway nights when the kids would sleep over at their grandparents' house for a night or two. It's ironic how much I cherished time away from my children—until suddenly it wasn't by choice. That's when the "c" word became commonplace in our family's vocabulary. Custody. Or rather, "shared custody."

It sounds lovely and amicable, doesn't it? We've been taught that it's good to share. But in reality, it boils down to one word: separation. The reality of that separation looked like this: not tucking my kids into bed every night, not always having them at the Thanksgiving dinner table, sometimes not waking up on Christmas morning and seeing their excited faces or celebrating with them on their birthday. It meant a lot of back and forth and packing clothes and unpacking clothes and things falling through the cracks. It meant sharing when I didn't want to share. It meant letting go before I was ready to let to go.

It's difficult when the things (or people) of this world have forced you to give up things you aren't ready to give up. Perhaps it was a job that ended before you were ready. Or a relationship that came to end, even though you didn't want it to. You may even find yourself parting with money when it wasn't your choice. Or you've had to give up time with those you love. Maybe you've even given up the *people* you love. All of those things, like custody, require separation. You might even fight back over the loss, trying to redeem what was taken. That certainly has been the case for me. Over the years, I've gone through many a court battle over custody, which sometimes went my way, and which sometimes didn't, but always caused me great anxiety as I dealt with the court system. Yes, that "c" word left a bad taste in my mouth.

But it wasn't until I lost my son that I began to think of custody in a different light. Oh, trust me, I wasn't ready to let go of my baby full-time. Part-time custody was hard enough. It didn't seem fair that I only had fourteen years of being Joe's mom. Didn't I deserve more time? Hadn't I been a loving mother? If I'm being honest, I had (and have) a lot of those thoughts of entitlement, feeling like something, some*one* was taken from me. And that seemed horribly unfair.

But whether you lost a child, have a child, or have been a child, here is a simple truth that needs daily reminding: *we belong to the Lord.* Scripture is replete with reminders of our connection to our Father.

> *"It is He who made us, and we are His;*
> *we are His people, and the sheep of His pasture."*
> ~ Psalm 100:3

> *"Fear not, for I have redeemed you;*
> *I have called you by name, you are Mine."*
> ~ Isaiah 43:1

> *"And it is God who establishes us with you in Christ,*
> *and has anointed us, and who has also put His seal on us*
> *and given us His Spirit in our hearts as a guarantee."*
> ~ 2 Corinthians 1:21-22

But there is one verse that stands out, which had become my son's favorite. Not only did he choose it for his confirmation verse, but it's also the verse that is etched at his burial site to bear witness to all who Joe truly belonged to:

"See what great love the Father has lavished on us, that we should be called
children of God. And that is what we are!"
~ 1 John 3:1

And as Paul reminds us in Romans 8, *nothing* can separate us from the love of God. Oh, the devil tries daily and sin does its best, but when the God of the universe makes us His children through the waters of baptism, it means that we are His. Period. Which means, as much as I would like to say that Joe was *mine*, he really was—and is still—the Lord's. Even death couldn't separate him from his Creator.

The realization that it wasn't *me* who shared my son with God, but rather *God* who shared him with me turned that entitled attitude of mine to one of gratitude. But God didn't only share *my* son (and daughter) with me, He also shared *His* son, Jesus, with me. And with you. And with the entirety of mankind. You see, there's a completely different custody situation to consider when it comes to our relationship with Jesus. There was separation required between the Father and the Son, but only so there could be reuniting between the Father and us. Sin separated us. Christ united us. No longer will we be judged by the law, which we could not keep perfectly, but we will be judged by what Jesus did on the cross, and now we get to claim His death as our own. Through that death, Christ freed us from the imprisonment of sin. We are now saved by His grace and are His children through faith. Forever!

The day a judge declared that I received full-time custody of my daughter was an incredible moment. No more back-and-forth, no more missing sleep over her safety, no more separation. But it will never compare to the day that she became a full-time daughter of the King through baptism those many years ago, when God declared that nothing would be able to separate her from His love. Just like her brother, she is a child of God, redeemed and set free from sin. I'm still co-parenting her with God. And as for my precious saint who has gone before? He's experiencing the full-time care of His loving Father. Case closed.

PRAYER

Lord, How grateful I am that You make me Your own child through the waters of baptism! Thank you for sharing Your Son with me so that I would not be held in prison by my own sin. Not only do I share in the suffering and death of Jesus, but because of that, I now get to share in the riches of forgiveness and eternity with You! May my heart be filled with comfort and hope knowing that You will never let go of me. Amen.

REFLECTION

What does it mean to you to be a baptized child of God?
If you are not, consider how being a part of the family of God would be a blessing in your life.

There's No Place like Home

"For we know that if the earthly tent we live in is destroyed, we have a building from God, an eternal house in heaven, not built by human hands."

~ 2 Corinthians 5:1

There was something familiar about the smell as soon as I stepped out of the airport terminal. I closed my eyes and breathed in deeply. Maybe it was the humidity. Maybe it was the smell of freshly cut grass and boxelder trees. Or just maybe it smelled like…home. It definitely wasn't the smell of the dry desert I had left a few hours prior, but the sweet summer scent of my childhood home: Nebraska.

It wasn't merely the smells that made it seem like home. As I sped down the interstate, water towers and grain solos rose high above the landscape, marking the presence of yet another small community in the middle of seemingly nowhere. Endless rows of corn waved in the always-present Nebraska winds. Mom-and-pop businesses lined the streets of small-town USA. It was a place where everything seemed different, yet nothing had changed. I grew up in an idyllic Midwestern small town. The kind of town where you could see into everyone's backyard, play outdoors until the streetlights came on, and ride your bike across town in ten minutes flat.

As I drove past my childhood home, I noticed a "for sale" sign in the front yard. And as luck would have it (or perhaps divine timing), a realtor classmate of mine just happened to be showing the home to prospective buyers the next day. Graciously, her clients agreed to let us tag along on their tour and walk through the home. And although the flooring had been changed, the kitchen remodeled, and each room painted a different color, there were so many things that hadn't changed. The wood framing around each door. The same bathroom fixtures. The planter with hanging vines. But perhaps, most importantly, the pencil markings in the laundry room, noting my siblings' and my height through our childhood years. It was unmistakably a feeling of "home," even though I knew I didn't really belong there. The home wasn't really mine and hadn't been for twenty years.

The next day as I left my childhood hometown of 7700 people to fly back to my current hometown of 1.6 million, I felt torn. "Am I leaving home? Or am I going home?" I wondered. "Where *is* home, really?" I've lived in over a dozen homes since my childhood home in Nebraska. Some were dorm rooms. A few were apartments. One was a small starter homes, and there were homes that were quite spacious. But regardless of the size and location or the furniture or décor on the walls, "home" meant the place where the people I loved most lived.

All of that made perfect sense—until my son went to go "home" to be with Jesus. No longer were all my loves under the same roof. And never would they be again this side of heaven. My heart was split. My sense of "home" completely altered. A big part of me wanted to go to my heavenly home to be with my son. How could I be separated from him for such a long time? But I also couldn't be apart from my daughter here on earth. Again, the question of "Where *is* home, really?" nagged my brain and prompted me to re-evaluate *what* home really meant.

As it turns out, "home" is the shelter in which one resides, but it's also the place where our primary "affections are centered" (thanks, dictionary.com). That certainly explained my feelings of being torn. I had two children in two different homes. But, perhaps what I needed to consider was not my definition of home and its location, but the location of my affections.

It's so easy to focus our devotion and love on those we feel close to, isn't it? Whether we do so with our children or our spouses or our parents or our friends, our affections become directed at those tangible relationships we can see or feel or hear most often. But as Christians, consider who desires to be the center of our *primary* affections. Oh, we know the answer to that Sunday School question, don't we? But the reality is that we don't always make our relationship with Jesus a priority. We get busy. We make excuses. We fit Him in whenever we happen to have the time. We forget that we're merely "in" the world, and act like we're "of" it.

However, there has never been a day when Jesus has not centered His affections around you. Or me. He has never desired to be apart from us for even a moment. He left his perfect home of heaven to enter our sinful world and live a perfect life. He gave up His childhood home to begin a ministry of teaching, healing, and loving. He could have returned to His home with the Father when He hung on the cross, but He chose to stay there, so that He could be home with us forever. Then He went back home to heaven to prepare a place for us. And even though it seems that we are separated from Him while we are on this earth, He continues to make *us* His dwelling place when He sends the Holy Spirit to live in our hearts. Because Jesus' primary affections are centered around *us*, that means our current home is the same as our future one: in eternity with our Savior.

Knowing that heaven is our true home and this earth is not means that everything we experience here is temporary. Our grief is temporary. Our pain is temporary. Our waiting is temporary. Our struggles are temporary. Even our earthly joys are temporary. But one day, we will have unending joy in our forever home. A home that was bought not with cash or a home loan, but with the blood of Jesus, who doesn't merely give us the keys and walk away, but who *is* the key.

PRAYER

Lord, I am so grateful that You have won for me an eternal home in heaven. When I hold on to the things of this world, remind me that all of it is temporary. Thank You that even my deepest grief and struggles are not forever and that one day I will rejoice in the presence of the saints and my Savior! Amen.

REFLECTION

What do you consider to be your home? How does knowing that earth is temporary and heaven is eternal affect your perspective on your trials?

_____

_____

_____

_____

_____

Unknown

"And You have searched me, Lord, and You know me.
You know when I sit and when I rise; You perceive my thoughts from afar.
You discern my going out and my lying down; You are familiar with all my ways.
Before a word is on my tongue, You, Lord, know it completely.
You hem me in behind and before, and You lay your hand upon me."

~ Psalm 139:1–4

Back-to-school time can mean many things: summer vacations have wrapped up, the weather begins to get a little cooler (well, except for those of us in the desert) and you can actually buy a pack of Crayola markers for under two dollars. But it also means school picture time is fast-approaching. It's when the curling irons come out, the fancy hair bows are put into place, and the hair gel attempts to tame the wildest of locks.

At the beginning of his freshman year, I remember *begging* my teenage son to use at least *some* product in his hair on school picture day. I made sure his favorite Arizona Cardinals football shirt was laundered and reminded him to *smile* and not try to be all cool-looking. As he got out of the car that day in the high school drop-off line, I would have never guessed that would be his last Monday here on earth, let alone his last school picture day.

Several weeks after he died, I got a phone call from the high school, saying Joe's school photos were waiting at the front desk to be picked up. In the midst of my grief, I had completely forgotten he had even had them done. As I walked into the school lobby to pick up the photos, I barely made eye contact with the school secretary. She quietly handed me the envelope and said, "We're all so sorry for your loss." I nodded my thanks and with tears in my eyes, made it to the car before I broke down sobbing. As I slowly pulled out the photos in the envelope, staring back at me with tears in *his* eyes, was my sweet boy.

The photo struck me as odd. Joe almost always took great photos. But there was no denying that this photo was different. He clearly had been sad on this day, and at this moment when the picture was taken. But why? What had happened? Did someone make fun of him? Was he not feeling well? Had he been upset about a grade he got? My mind went back to the day I picked him up after picture day. I asked him how it went. He said it was fine. There was nothing I could recollect that would give me any insight into why that picture showed the tears in his eyes.

There are many difficult aspects to grief, but perhaps one of the hardest is wrestling with the unknown. From wanting to know what life would have been like had we not experienced tragedy to wishing we could have insight into the thoughts and actions of our loved one we miss so much, we struggle with the not knowing. Or perhaps we don't understand why we have to suffer and we ask God those "why" questions, but never seem to get an answer. Not only does the past become a huge unknown, but so does the future. We wonder what life would have been like if our loved one *hadn't* died.

But more than struggling with the unknown, we struggle with simply missing the one we love. We miss being with them. We miss seeing them. We miss touching them and talking to them. We just miss walking through life with them. But we also miss what will forever be unknown to us. Maybe like me, you look at pictures of people doing life with their loved ones while your life seems unfairly empty. Or you see your friends celebrate an anniversary that you will never reach. Or hold a baby that you've been relentlessly trying to have. When we focus on what we're missing or what's been taken – or even what hasn't been given, we're left angry, jealous, and resentful.

I get it. Because I have been there so many times over the years. I dwell on the unknown past of "why" and the unknown future of "why not." In those moments when I am tempted to make it about me and my losses is the precise moment I need to take my eyes off the unknowns and turn them to my God, who is known. And when I do, God graciously inundates my heart and mind with what He *has* made known to me about who He is. Despite the unknowns in my world.

Although I will never know God in all His fullness, here is what I *know* about who He is, because His Word says He is.

God is good.

"For the Lord is good and His love endures forever; His faithfulness continues through all generations."

~ Psalm 100:5

God is love.

"And so we know and rely on the love God has for us. God is love. Whoever lives in love lives in God, and God in them."

~ 1 John 4:16

God is faithful.

"Because of the Lord's great love we are not consumed, for His compassions never fail. They are new every morning; great is Your faithfulness."

~ Lamentations 3:22-23

God is with me.

"The Lord your God is with you, the Mighty Warrior who saves. He will take great delight in you; in His love He will no longer rebuke you, but will rejoice over you with singing."

~ Zephaniah 3:17

God has a plan.

"For I know the plans I have for you," declares the Lord, "plans to prosper you and not to harm you, plans to give you hope and a future."

~ Jeremiah 29:11

God gives hope.

"Yes, my soul, find rest in God; my hope comes from Him."

~ Psalm 62:5

God's promises never fail.

*"You know with all your heart and soul that not one of all the
good promises the Lord your God gave you has failed.
Every promise has been fulfilled; not one has failed."*

~ Joshua 23:14

Cling to those promises, my friends. God's plans may not be for us
to fully know or even understand, but here's good news: the circumstances and trials we have walked through, are walking through, and
will walk through in this life will *never* change who God is. And God's
intimate knowledge of *us*—good, bad, or ugly—will never change how
much He loves us. We may never have the answers about an unknown
past and we certainly have a future on this earth that remains
unknown. But we know how it all ends because Jesus defeated sin,
death, and the devil. As a dear friend of mine often says with complete
assurance, "I know that I know that I *know* my Redeemer lives."

Most likely, I will never know the reason for those tears in my
son's eyes on that freshman picture day. But I do know that God knew.
He saw it all. From Joe's first breath to his last, nothing was a surprise
to Him. And neither were my tears in the parking lot as I looked at
those pictures. Having a God who knows, who sees, and who loves
will always be enough. In the words of another dear Christian lady,
Corrie Ten Boom, "Never be afraid to trust an unknown future to a
known God."

PRAYER

Lord, there are so many unknowns about the past as well as
the future. As hard as it is for me to live in the unknown, give
me the assurance that You know everything and see everything from Your perfect perspective. Remind me constantly
of who You are—loving, faithful, kind, and good. May Your
promises to be with me and have a plan for my life sustain me
until I am forever in Your presence. Amen.

REFLECTION

What is one "unknown" you wish you had the answer to? What is one "known" about God that brings you comfort?

_____

_____

_____

_____

_____

How Much Longer???

"My Father is always at His work to this day, and I too am working."

~ John 5:17

"Are we there yet?" I asked for the millionth time from the back-seat of our 1972 AMC Hornet as it rambled down the interstate. I was impatient to get out of the stuffy car and run around. Crammed in the backseat with my siblings and no air conditioning, I carefully peeled up each leg that was stuck to the vinyl seats. I leaned over into the front seat and whispered in my dad's ear, "How much longer?" It didn't matter the destination: lunch at McDonald's, the nearest rest area, Grandma's house, or the next Motel 6. *I just wanted to get there.* Because at the end of the road, there was the hope and promise of something better than my present circumstances. Perhaps it was a Happy Meal, a cool swimming pool, a homemade meal, the freedom to run around, or simply my grandparents' waiting arms.

It was on those long family road trips that I developed a love for maps. I'm certain my parents were exhausted from my endless questioning of "how much longer," so they spent the time teaching me how to read a map. I learned to calculate the mileage between two exit numbers, look for alternative routes, and find cities that started with each letter of the alphabet. I'd often pour through the atlas and make up games that involved guessing the distance between cities or the population of a certain city. But even with the distraction of maps, endless card games, and hunting for different license plates, I never failed to continually ask the question, "HOW MUCH LONGER???"

Fast-forward several decades later and I find myself asking the same question. Not to my dad from the backseat of a '72 AMC

Hornet, but to my heavenly Father from…well, the front seat of my present circumstances. It seems like there are some prayers I have been praying for a long time. It might be asking God for a certain situation to change in my life. Or it might be a prayer for a loved one to be healed. Or it might be wondering just how long the pain of losing a child will last.

But regardless of *what* I'm praying about, the fact remains that I feel like I'm praying the same prayers over and over and over again. I've used different words. I've prayed at different times. I've prayed with different people. I've been in my bed, on the road, at the table, on my knees, and guess what? I still find myself praying the *same prayers*. And it's in those moments of frustration, when I feel like I must be doing it wrong or I need to be doing something differently, that I find myself literally throwing my hands up to God in frustration and crying out, "HOW MUCH LONGER???"

And I know I'm in good company, certainly with many of you, but also with those who have penned those same words in Scripture. Well, they maybe haven't written those *exact* words, but they come pretty close. The Bible is replete with "how long" questions, but none so much as in the book of Psalms. Here's just a few:

> *"My soul is in deep anguish. How long, Lord, how long?"*
> ~ Psalm 6:3

> *"How long, Lord? Will you hide Yourself forever?"*
> ~ Psalm 89:46

> *"Relent, Lord! How long will it be? Have compassion on Your servants."*
> ~ Psalm 90:13

> *"How long must Your servant wait?"*
> ~ Psalm 119:84

And then there's my personal favorite:

> *"How long, O Lord? Will You forget me forever?*
> *How long will You hide Your face from me?*
> *How long must I take counsel in my soul*

and have sorrow in my heart all the day?
How long shall my enemy be exalted over me?"
~ Psalm 13:1-2

Yep. You read that right. There were *four* "how long" phrases in just *two* verses. Feeling in good company now? Perhaps like David, there are times when it feels like God has abandoned us, or as if He is silent. Inattentive. Unmoving. Doesn't He hear our pleas? Our desires? Our desperate prayers on behalf of those we love? Why isn't He choosing to act? Has He forgotten us? If only we could know a timeline for the "how long," maybe we could endure whatever it is we're going through.

And yet, therein lies the issue, doesn't it? There's no map we can pull out to see just how much further we need to go. We don't know how much longer our trials will last—or if we'll even get to the end. If we did, would we even have need to go to God in prayer and cry out for help and deliverance? Or would we simply just mark off the days on the calendar until our trial was over?

So what are we to do when the wait seems long and unbearable? We can learn a thing or two about the verses that follow David's excessive "how long" questions. In the very next verse he says, *"Give light to my eyes,"* meaning, "Give me a new perspective on this situation, God, because I can't see what You can." He wants a new vision of the one he's currently experiencing. I don't know about you, but sometimes having a different perspective on a long wait can make a big difference. Whether it's praying for contentment or finding the blessings in hardship, a new outlook can help get us to the other side.

From my childlike view, every passing mile our family drove didn't seem to bring us any closer to our destination. But as I grew and matured, I had a different perspective. I realized that there was value in the waiting. I learned to read mileage signs and markers. I learned to navigate an atlas with ease. I learned there was value in talking and playing games, which strengthened my family relationships. And now, even though I know God isn't merely silent, but is working in my waiting, I'm recognizing that waiting isn't just about suffering through my circumstances, but watching what God has, is, and will do through them.

It's in the waiting that we can remember all God *has* done so faithfully in the past for us and for those we love. And it's also in the waiting that God is fulfilling His purpose of bringing people into a closer relationship with Him and working out salvation for those who are far off. And like David who initially complained, "how long," our remembrance of God's faithfulness can produce praise as it did for him:

"But I trust in Your unfailing love; my heart rejoices in Your salvation.
I will sing the Lord's praise, for He has been good to me."
~ Psalm 13:5-6

May it be the fervent cry of our heart to follow up our complaining and whining prayers of "how long" with praise to our God for all He has done, is doing, and will do in our lives. Our Father has the road map, and He knows the way. The road of waiting may be long, but there is incredible hope and promise for a future in heaven, which is infinitely better than our present circumstances here on earth. In that waiting, let us watch for all the ways God is working to bring us and others deeper into a relationship with Him. And eventually, we will make it to our heavenly destination, where we will joyfully jump out of the grave and run straight into our Father's waiting arms.

PRAYER

Lord, You hear without fail the prayers I speak aloud and the ones that are in my heart. Give me the assurance that not only are You listening to those prayers, but You are always working to accomplish Your will through them in Your own perfect timing. Help me see the ways You are at work as I wait and fill my lungs with prayers of praise for all You have done for me. Amen.

REFLECTION

What is your "how long" cry to God? How has God shown His faithfulness in your wait?

_____

_____

_____

_____

_____

Traditioooooon......TRADITION!

"I tell you, I will not drink from this fruit of the vine from now on until that day when I drink it new with you in my Father's kingdom."

~ Matthew 26:29

When my grandmother passed away many years ago, all her earthly possessions were laid out on eight-foot folding tables in the musty, wood-paneled community center of the small Missouri town she had last lived in. Her seven children got first pick of their mother's treasures, and after that, we grandchildren were allowed to peruse the tables for items by which to remember our grandma. I knew I didn't want any of her jewelry, trinkets, needlepoint projects, kitchenware, clothing, or piano music. There was only one thing I desperately wanted, and like a frantic garage-saler on a mission, I made a beeline straight for it: a 1940's Universal Climax food and meat chopper. "Really???" you may ask. "Of all your grandmother's things, you'd pick an old, rusty, crank-handled food chopper?"

Absolutely. But not because that actual item holds any real value or meaning for me. I don't even have any memories of my grandma using it. Rather, my mother had one just like it and ever since I can remember, that's how she made the traditional Thanksgiving cranberry relish every year. She would cut up the apples and peel the oranges and rinse the cranberries in the green plastic colander. And then she'd call my brother and sister and me into the kitchen to take turns loading the food chopper and turning the crank, while the mashed-up fruit came out the front end. It didn't matter how old we got. It was just something we always did the day before Thanksgiving.

That food chopper symbolized something we all hold on to dearly around any holiday season: *tradition*. Having that food chopper meant that even if I wouldn't be home for the holidays, I would still be able to eat cranberry relish on Thanksgiving. Furthermore, I'd be able to pass down that tradition of making and eating the mashed-up fruit to my own children.

Some of us love that word—tradition. We're comforted by the fact that each year, something—or maybe many things—will be the same. We don't have to make decisions about what to eat, what to do, or who to be with, because there's a consistency each time a particular holiday or event rolls around. People ask us what our favorite traditions are and we proudly reply with, "Well, we *always...*" or *"Every year, we...."*

And while traditions are all good and well, there are some of us who may have some difficulty hearing that word, particularly if our lives have been radically changed due to loss. While Thanksgiving 2011 seemed "traditional" in every sense of the word, Thanksgiving 2012 saw my then-husband pack up his clothes and leave our family while I stood in the driveway holding two crying children. Thanksgiving 2013 meant having no dad at the table. Thanksgiving 2014 meant going solo to the family dinner while my kids were with their dad. But it was Thanksgiving 2016 that meant never having *two* children at the table again. How I longed for the days of "normal," rather than constant change. Where was the familiar? The traditional?

Maybe it hasn't been about Thanksgiving for you, but Christmas. Or an anniversary. Or a birthday. You look around that table and think, "What happened?" A familiar face from the year before isn't there. Nothing seems the same. If you're anything like me, you wish you could go back and have just one more "traditional" time around the table. If only you had known.

But God did. And He knew our hearts would long for tradition, with all the foods of comfort, and to be with those with love. But more importantly to be with the *One* we love.

And we do, in fact, get to share in a very familiar, very traditional meal with our family. A meal that traces its roots back thousands of years as God's people were delivered out of Egypt and spared the death of their firstborn sons. A meal that was celebrated year after year from generation to generation to remind them of that deliverance. A meal that Christ shared with His disciples the night before His crucifixion. A meal with the traditional foods of bread and wine that we get to share with our brothers and sisters in Christ. A meal that means we now are delivered from the bondage and sin and eternal death. And it is because of the sacrifice of God's Son that means one day we'll sit at a different table and share in the heavenly feast that never ends.

That's a feast my son now enjoys. Someday I'll join him at the table, just as we used to years ago. And I imagine, I'll see you there, too, as we raise our glasses and break bread with all the saints—and our Savior, who paid the price for such a precious feast.

I can't think of a better tradition to start.

PRAYER

Lord, I am filled with thanksgiving when I reflect on all You have done for me on the cross! Thank You that because of that sacrifice, I will get to enjoy the feast that never ends at Your heavenly table. As time passes and traditions change, remind me that You are constant in Your love and faithfulness. Amen.

REFLECTION

What traditions have changed for you over the years? What does it mean to you to share in the meal of Communion with your brothers and sisters in Christ?

_____

_____

_____

_____

This Too Shall Pass

"Heaven and earth will pass away, but My words will never pass away."

~ Matthew 24:35

When we were in the throes of parenting young children, my sister and I would often call each other for support. It didn't matter what we were dealing with—colicky infants, teething babies, or tantrum-filled toddlers—our conversation always concluded with this consoling phrase: This too shall pass. It served to remind us that even though the current situation we were in seemed endless, there was hope that it wouldn't last forever. Eventually the colic would stop. The tooth would pop through the gum. The tantrums would subside. We continued to use that phrase throughout our kids' childhoods when things seemed more trivial than cutting a tooth. Academic struggles. Issues with friends. Defiant teenage behavior. Trust me, there were days when it would have been easier to deal with an over-tired toddler.

We can look back on those temporary seasons now with a smile. Because, indeed, those seemingly difficult times eventually did pass. By no means did parenting become easier. It just became different with the passing of time. The hardships were different. But so were the joys. Which I'm realizing, is not dissimilar to the journey of grief many of us find ourselves on.

Perhaps you are in—or can remember—that early season of grief. The emotions are still raw. You find it hard to grasp the new reality of your life. You struggle to get out of bed. You're angry at God. You don't get it. Allow yourself grace in this season. It may take some time, but *this too shall pass.*

Maybe it's been a few years and you've moved to a place of acceptance, but it's still hard. You still wish things could have been different. You have good days and bad days. Sometimes you might feel like you're back at the beginning. But the pain of your loss isn't quite as sharp as in those early days and weeks. Allow yourself grace in this season. I don't know when, *but this too shall pass.*

You survive one year. Then two. Then maybe even five. Or ten. Is grief still there? Absolutely. I am quite certain that the grief itself will *never* pass. But it will look and feel different. The hardships may not be the same as they were initially, but joy slowly creeps in. Allow yourself grace in this season to feel both sadness *and* joy.

Jesus shares a lengthy discussion in the book of Matthew about the end times with His disciples. He reveals that there will be a season of devastation on the earth before He returns. He refers to wars and earthquakes and famines and false prophets and persecution. Doesn't sound very pleasant, does it? I'm sure we could add our own season of devastation to the list: cancer, unemployment, divorce, miscarriage, death. But as we walk through various seasons of trials and difficulties, we can take comfort in the fact that one thing will never change: the Word of God. Whether we open Scripture in times of sorrow or anxiousness or frustration, we receive comfort and joy and hope— and the promise that one day, they will pass. Because grace had been shown.

We know it to be true because that is exactly what the Word of God says happened. Grace was shown in the garden of Eden when sin entered the world. Grace was shown when a tiny little baby was born in a smelly, animal-filled Bethlehem stable, lived on this earth as one of us, and died on a hill called Calvary. Grace was shown as our lifeless Savior hung on a cross and was placed in a tomb. But, most of all, grace was shown the moment the stone was rolled away from that very tomb on Easter morning and the resurrected Jesus appeared to His disciples. Because grace means we got something we didn't deserve. Or rather, *who* we didn't deserve: a Savior to rescue us from our sin and struggles on this earth.

I don't know what season you find yourself in today. Perhaps you are anxious about an unknown future. If so, know that you can

"Cast all your anxiety on Him, because He cares for you."
~ 1 Peter 5:7

If you are lonely, be assured that,

"The Lord Himself goes before you and will be with you;
He will never leave you nor forsake you...."
~ Deuteronomy 31:8

If you are grieving, be confident you have a God who is

"...the Father of all compassion...who comforts us in all our troubles...."
~ 2 Corinthians 1:3-4

If you are overwhelmed and exhausted by the circumstances of your life, you have a God that says,

"Come to me, all who weary and burdened, and I will give you rest."
~ Matthew 11:28

You can be confident that you have a God that will carry you through each and every challenging season until it ends. And it will pass. That's the beauty of seasons: they don't last forever. But all the promises above? They have never and will never change.

Let us allow God to determine the course of our seasons, and as they pass, may we ask Him to reveal to us all that He is, which has not changed since the world began. Constantly caring for us, despite our changing emotions. Constantly providing for our every need. Constantly by our side in all things. Constantly comforting us in our grief. Constantly inviting us to rest in Him. Constantly showing us grace each day. May the constancy our Lord daily provides give us strength, peace, and joy until the never-ending season of heaven is ours forever!

PRAYER

Lord, no matter the season I find myself in, remind me that You love me and that You are always with me, taking care of my every need. In seasons of joy, show me how I can extend Your blessings to those around me. In seasons of hardship, send others to minster to me of Your love. I praise You for sending Jesus to die in my place, so that one day I could be with You in a season of never-ending joy and peace. Amen.

REFLECTION

What "season" do you find yourself in now? How can you show yourself grace during this time? What has God taught you about Himself in this season?

Clothed in Anxiety

*"I delight greatly in the Lord; my soul rejoices in my God.
For He has clothed me with the garments of salvation
and arrayed me in a robe of His righteousness..."*

~ Isaiah 61:10

"I have nothing to wear!"

We've all heard those words before. Maybe from a child who doesn't have that "just right" outfit to go hang with her friends. Maybe from a spouse who feels like they've worn it all before and wants something new and fresh. Or maybe, those words have even come out of our own mouths. And truth be told, it's not that there's *nothing* to wear. It's just that what we do have hanging in our closet doesn't meet our satisfaction.

I'll admit I've said this on more than one occasion. Okay, maybe a hundred occasions. I'm someone who likes to be appropriately dressed for any and all possible events, because it's an awful feeling to stand out for not wearing the right thing. (There might have been some possible emotional scarring from showing up to my freshman homecoming dance in *not* the right outfit, but I digress.) It's also an embarrassment to show up in the same outfit as someone, only to discover they wore it better. Yes, it's true that I've hemmed and hawed about what to wear. But that was before.

Before the unthinkable happened and my son went to be with Jesus.

After that horrible day. I'd find myself getting out of the shower, heart pounding, and staring for several minutes at my clothes hanging in the closet. I'd have to sit on the bed, think some more, breathe in and out slowly, and then try again. My eyes would fill with tears. I just couldn't seem to make a decision. The *right* decision. It was crazy. Insane. Completely irrational. What was wrong with me? What I didn't realize was that for the first time in my life, I was experiencing anxiety. You may think I'm crazy, but if you understand anything about anxiety, you know it takes on some very odd little quirks, which make absolutely no sense and defies all logic.

I tried to fix my issues on my own. I'd attempt to pick out my clothes the night before, only to find that I hated my choice when I woke up in the morning. I read Bible verses about anxiety and not worrying about what to wear. I prayed for God to take my anxiety away. But in the end, I finally went to a doctor, who was able to pre-scribe some medication for me to take to help with all these anxious feelings I was experiencing. And sure enough, after a few months, I mostly got to a place of peace and calm in my mind when it came to choosing clothes.

But here's the real honest, ugly-truth deal: I still struggle. Daily. And not just with getting dressed, but with other anxieties, too. For the most part, I've learned ways to cope with them now so that I can still function. Some days I function better than others. (And if I ever get to the point again where I need some help medically...well, I've learned that's okay, too.) I still read Scripture. I still sing songs of praise. I still pray and ask God to take my anxieties away. But I also am aware that God may be choosing to not do so yet. Maybe not for a long time. Or maybe not even while I walk this earth.

Which leads me to believe that maybe there's a purpose in all this struggle. A purpose I don't know right now.

I do know that God is using this season to teach me something. For someone who is incredibly logical and rational, I've learned that anxiety doesn't always make sense. I've learned to be gentle with myself and know my limitations. I've learned God provides help when I need it. I've become more compassionate towards those who deal with anxiety and am able to share my own struggles with it. I don't have a solution. I don't have a happy ending, but I do have this encouragement:

> *"My grace is sufficient for you, for My power is made perfect in weakness.*
> *Therefore I will boast all the more gladly about my weaknesses,*
> *so that Christ's power may rest on me. That is why, for Christ's sake,*
> *I delight in weaknesses, in insults, in hardships, in persecutions, in difficulties.*
> *For when I am weak, then I am strong."*
> ~ 2 Corinthians 12:9-10

I can't tell you when anxiety will no longer affect me. I can't tell you how to get rid of anxiety. Or depression. Or addiction. Or whatever it is you're struggling with. But I can tell you this: there are a lot of things that weaken me daily. That have weakened me in the past. Big things. Things that *should* have broken me. And I dare to say, that there's a good chance there are things you've dealt with and deal with that should have broken you, too. But it is through the power and strength and grace of God *alone* that allows us to still function and walk this journey of life.

So, friends, when people claim you are strong, know that it is Christ's strength they see and not your own. When people wonder how you can still smile and laugh despite your circumstances, know that it is because of hope in Christ that your heart can still be joyful. When you appear resilient, know that it is only because of the power in Christ in you that allows you to keep putting one foot in front of the other. And when others wonder about the great love you have for those around you, know that it is because of the example of Christ's love on the cross that you have any to give. The only things we can offer this world are our weaknesses and brokenness. But Christ offers us so much more! He offers strength and hope and forgiveness and love and peace to our aching souls. He wrote it with His own blood, shed for us on the cross, so that one day we would be able to have a life dressed in His righteousness alone and stand faultless before His throne.

Choosing what to wear on that day isn't a decision we'll ever have to make. The choice was our Father's, who willingly sent Jesus to die for us and who willingly chose us as His children. Anything we could have chosen on our own would not have met God's satisfaction. But wearing Christ's robe of righteousness means being dressed perfectly for the occasion. And don't worry if we're wearing the same outfit. Nobody wore it better than Jesus.

PRAYER

Lord, You know me so intimately and see all my struggles and shortcomings. And yet You love me with an everlasting love. If it be Your will, please heal me from anxiety and all the other emotions I struggle with. And if not, teach me something about who You are in the midst of it. When others see my struggles, let them see You and Your strength in my life. Amen.

REFLECTION

What have you struggled with that you've tried to fix on your own? How has Christ's power in your weakness given you strength?

_____

_____

_____

_____

_____

Perpetually Sunday

"Why do you look for the living among the dead?
He is not here; He has risen!"

~ Luke 24:6

I love Saturdays. I may even go as far to say that I *live* for Saturdays. Even my former students could tell you that. Whenever we'd pull out the little pink card on Friday at calendar time that said, "Saturday" and place it in the "tomorrow" slot, my kids would all shout, "Your favorite day!" Ah, yes…Saturday. It's the one day I don't have to set an alarm and can lounge in bed. I can move at my own speed and do things that need to get done without the stress of another workday to follow. I can run to Target at eleven in the morning if my heart so desires or take a hike at four in the afternoon. There's something very expectant about an upcoming Saturday, as if anything is possible.

But there's one Saturday each year that feels a bit different than the rest. It's that day after Good Friday when you leave in somber silence—and the day before Easter when the "Hallelujahs" and the "He is Risens" are about to burst forth. It's a confusing mix of emotions. Should I be mourning Jesus' death on that Saturday? Should I be excited about the day to come tomorrow? I usually don't give a lot of thought to the Saturday in between, but I recently was wondering what that first Holy Saturday might have looked like for those left in the wake of Jesus' death.

Knowing it was the Sabbath, it surely would have been a Saturday of rest. But I imagine it was also a very still, quiet Saturday as well. One with few words and probably many tears. Or perhaps it was a day of utter shock and confusion from everything they had witnessed the day before. A day of wondering, "Now what?" A day in which those who loved Jesus deeply had no idea how they would move past their grief and have hope for their future.

I know that day well. And if you've suffered any kind of loss, I know you do, too.

Living with grief is a lot like that first Holy Saturday. It doesn't matter if it's been two days, two months, two years, or twenty since the loss. The pain and anguish from the past is always remembered. There's still shock some days. Times of overwhelming sadness. Many questions. We're like the disciples on the day after Jesus' death, not understanding what just happened and how we'll ever move on... stuck in a perpetual Holy Saturday.

But unlike the disciples, we know what's coming, because we've read the next chapter of the story. It's easy for us to think about what we would have said to those who loved Jesus following His death. We'd burst into the room and say with confidence, "I know you're sad, but you won't be for long. Just wait till you see what happens tomorrow!" Because we *know* what's to come. But the disciples didn't. Despite Jesus' prediction of His own death, they must have thought that death was more likely than life. They thought all had been lost. They thought it was the end. They had lost their Savior. Their friend. Their very hope. They saw that loss with their very own eyes.

It's easy to have hope when you know how the story ends. But having hope in the middle of the story is much harder.

I remember a few weeks after Joe died having the desire to find a group of parents who understood what I was going through. My GriefShare group was great, but no one had lost a child and it was hard to relate to anyone else's experience. So I went online and found a prominent Facebook group for those who had lost children. I found myself getting not only sucked into the stories, but into the grief others were experiencing. The posts in that group were often overwhelming, describing how months and even years after the death of their child, parents were often crying daily, inconsolable, and unable to get out of bed. I wondered if this was what was in store for me. Would I ever be able to experience joy again? Was my life doomed to one of inability to function and participate in life? It was as if these people were living in a perpetual Saturday post-death, but with no knowledge of the resurrection that was just around the corner. I wanted to burst into these people's homes and say, "I know you're sad now, but don't you know what's to come?"

Because I know how the story ends. You see, for the believer, there is one marked difference from that Saturday when Jesus lay in the ground and every Saturday after that. And it's this: *Our story doesn't end with grief. It ends with joy and victory over death.* While the unbeliever looks backwards to death, the believer looks forward to the assurance of life that God has promised and that Christ has won.

Hope is not lost, because we *do* know what's coming. We know there *is* a resurrection. We know there *is* the defeat of death. We know there *is* a Savior who did not stay in the grave. Knowing this, believing this, hoping in this truth is what sustains us in the perpetual Saturday that follows loss. It changes our hearts from grieving *without* hope to grieving *with* joy, knowing what's to come. It fills our hearts with an expectancy—because now *everything* has been made possible through Jesus' suffering and death. Forgiveness, life, hope, joyful reunions— it's all ours! And not just on Saturday, but every day.

PRAYER

Lord, help me not stay stuck in my grief and on thoughts of the past. When those thoughts seek to overwhelm me, remind me that my story didn't end with Your death, but with Your resurrection. And that joyful day was the beginning of new life for all who believe in You. Fill me with Your hope and give me joy in the midst of my mourning. Amen.

REFLECTION

In what circumstances has it been difficult to have hope?
How does knowing your story ends in victory over death affect your
hope on hard days?

The Recliner on the Sidewalk

"Come to Me, all who are weary and burdened
and I will give you rest."

~ Matthew 11:28

A few years after my encounter with the toilet on the sidewalk, I found myself thrust into yet another "toilet" season I didn't see coming. It was definitely a season which fueled my anxiety, caused unreasonable fear and panic, and precipitated the need to leave my home of several years to move into the necessary school district for my daughter's high school years. June became a flurry of legal dealings, apartment hunting, online postings to sell half our furniture, garage sale organization, and moving. It was a series of tasks that required just as much emotional energy as physical energy, primarily because it required letting go of "Joe's room" and the last home he lived in. How would I be able to sell his furniture and move to a place he had never lived before? I had moved into this home six years ago with two kids. How could I leave with only one? My heart and mind struggled with this new reality.

It was at the height of all this chaos that once again, I found myself putting in the earbuds, cranking up the worship music and walking around the neighborhood to sort out and process all the change. As I tried to calm myself and prepare for what I knew was going to be a particularly tough day ahead, I happened to look up in just enough time to see it before I walked smack into it. You guessed it.

The recliner on the sidewalk.

Right in my path. Directly in front of me. After six years of living in my lower middle-class neighborhood, I can't say I was that surprised to encounter such an item sitting out there on the side-walk. (I still attest that you could furnish a small apartment by simply walking around the block.) But this recliner, much like the toilet, was dead center in my path, facing me head-on. I stood there for a while, chuckling to myself. "Okay, God. Surely You have something to tell me," I said out loud. But as I continued on my way, back home to the daunting to-do list and the fears and worries that overwhelmed me, that recliner (or what God was trying to tell me *through* the recliner) quickly left my thoughts.

Even after all the packing and moving and unpacking, I still felt restless about what the future held. Perhaps many of you know what it's like to experience something traumatic, which makes you realize that now *anything* is possible—particularly, anything *negative*. Just because the unthinkable has already happened, who's to say that everything else in life will go smoothly? Perhaps your fears defy logic, but your brain must prepare for any given situation, right? And that's where my brain was. Preparing for the worst and desperately trying to find some peace.

I had tried finding that elusive rest in all kinds of ways...sleeping without setting an alarm, binge-watching Netflix, playing games, lounging in the pool, aimlessly scrolling on Pinterest and Facebook whenever my heart desired. I even thought that getting away for a little vacation to the mountains and away from the to-do lists would do the trick. But even that didn't accomplish any type of relief from the anxiety and fears that plagued me.

So...why didn't my heart and mind feel at rest? What was I doing wrong? And as I often do much too late in the game, I opened my Bible app in desperation. Perhaps Scripture had some answers for me.

"Whoever dwells in the shelter of the Most High
will rest in the shadow of the Almighty."
~ Psalm 91:1

"My Presence will go with you, and I will give you rest."
~ Exodus 33:14

"Come to Me, all who are weary and burdened and I will give you rest."
~ Matthew 11:28

"Those are great verses, God, but where is this elusive rest you keep referencing? I can't find it! How can I get some of that for myself?" I prayed with frustration. Maybe God and I had different definitions of "rest." I wasn't desperate for physical rest, but rest from my thoughts about the future.

As I went about my day, the words from Matthew 11 kept playing over and over in my head. *"Come to Me, all who are weary and burdened and I will give you rest."* And in doing so, my thoughts shifted from focusing on "weary and burdened and rest"—words all about me—to the first part of the verse, *"Come to ME."*

It didn't say "Come to the mountains" or "Come to Facebook" or "Come to the swimming pool" or "Come to Netflix" to find rest. It says, "Come to Me." It was as if God was saying, "Remember that recliner I put in your path when you were overwhelmed? That was my reminder to you to *rest*. To rest in *Me*, not in the things of this world. Stop walking and talking and thinking and worrying. It's accomplishing nothing! Come sit in the comfy, familiar recliner of *My* love, put your feet up, lean back and look up. Take a break from this world and spend time with *Me*. Pray to *Me*, talk to *Me*, worship *Me*, listen to *My* Word. I am your rest from everything this world throws at you. Your problems are temporary, but my love is forever."

It sounds so basic, so simple, doesn't it? Just pray, read the Bible, worship, and focus on God to find rest. Check! Done! But let me be honest here. If all we need to do to achieve true rest in God relies solely on us, we will fall short. Every time. Friends, the reason we can even *come* to God, whether it be in prayer or the Word or in worship is because *He* first came to *us* in the human form of His Son. Jesus came to this earth to relieve the burden of sin and death and everything else that overwhelms us just so we could have access to the Father forever. Not because we deserved it, but because of His great love for us and His great desire to be with us in *eternal* rest one day.

That eternal rest is sounding better and better with each passing day, isn't it? But until that day is here, we can still come to Him, shelter in the shadow of the Almighty, and find rest for our souls whenever we need it. It may not mean getting more sleep or having more time to watch Netflix. But soul rest is so much deeper and so much more satisfying. So sit down and put your feet up in the recliner of God's love and mercy.

And *rest*.

PRAYER

Lord, free me from my anxious thoughts and worries about the temporal matters of this world. Remind me to seek You in word and worship and prayer during those times. Thank You for Your many promises to be with me and to love me. May I rest in all Your promises when life gets overwhelming. Amen.

REFLECTION

What things do you do to find rest from the stresses and worries in your life? What does it look like for you to rest in the recliner of God's love and peace?

_____

_____

_____

_____

_____

Alterations

"Be still and know that I am God."

~ Psalm 46:10

S o, when's the big day?" The seamstress looked at me expectantly in the full-length mirror, waiting for me to give her an answer as she zipped up the back of my wedding gown. "Uhmm…we haven't set a date yet." I forced a smile on my face, and reassured myself that by the end of the alterations process I *surely* would be able to give her a more definitive answer. It had been nearly a year since I bought my dress and even though there was really no wedding date on the horizon, I wanted to be ready. *Just in case.*

When I bought my dress, the sales consultant was certain that not much work needed to be done. However, upon my first visit to the seamstress, it was obvious that many alterations would need to be made. The hem would clearly need to be taken up several inches. The top was too loose and falling off my shoulders. Things weren't lining up in the chest area. I could clearly see *what* needed to be fixed. And yet, I didn't have slightest clue *how* it needed to get done. But Terry did.

"Oh, I'll just pin this here and cut this off here and restitch this here…" Her words were like a foreign language to me. I nodded in agreement with everything she said. I mean, it wasn't *my* job to tell Terry what to do. *She* was the master seamstress, not me. *She* was the one with all the tools, the thread, the needles and other supplies. *She* was the one with decades of sewing experience, where all I've mastered is how to sew on a button that came loose. I had no expertise in how to alter anything at all, let alone something as complicated as a wedding dress. My only job was to stand still, let her make the necessary alterations and then marvel at her handiwork. When I left each time, I had complete faith and trust that the next time I returned, the dress would fit even better than before.

And it did. Because the master seamstress knew exactly what needed to be done. And had the ability to do it. Whenever I returned to her home for the next fitting, I could envision that maybe a wedding really *was* possible in the near future. But after driving away, my own personal circumstances would soon remind me that I was no closer to a wedding date now than I was when I bought the dress. My current situation seemed unchanging. Frustrating. Hopeless. Impossible. I could see *what* needed to be done, but I didn't know *how* to make it a reality. Or rather, how *God* was going to do it. Couldn't he just alter the course of my life if He wanted to?

It soon dawned on me that here I was, putting my complete faith and trust in an earthly seamstress to produce a beautifully altered gown...yet doubting and mistrusting my God, the Master Seamster, to produce beautifully altered circumstances for my life. Was it because I felt like He's taking too long? Or not moving in ways I think He should? Or rather, in the *time* I felt He should?

Dear friend, I am sure you, like me, have had times where you have felt impatient for God to make some grand alterations to your life. And I don't believe we're alone in that thought. So many times in Scripture, God's people were waiting for some circumstance to be changed and for God to bring them out of seemingly impossible situations. They, like us, might have *seen* what needed to be done, but had no clue how it would be accomplished.

Remember Sarah who waited for a child and was still barren at age ninety? Look what God did!

> *"Sarah said, 'God has brought me laughter,*
> *and everyone who hears about this will laugh with me.'*
> *And she added, 'Who would have said to Abraham that Sarah*
> *would nurse children? Yet I have borne him a son in his old age.'"*
> ~ Genesis 21:6–7

Remember the Israelites who waited hundreds of years to be delivered from slavery and found themselves standing before a sea, with Pharoah's army in pursuit? Look what God did!

"Then Moses stretched out his hand over the sea, and all that night the Lord drove the sea back with a strong east wind and turned it into dry land. The waters were divided, and the Israelites went through the sea on dry ground, with a wall of water on their right and on their left."
~ Exodus 14:21–22

Remember Daniel who waited all night in the lions' den, wondering if he'd still be alive in the morning? Look what God did!

"Daniel answered, 'May the king live forever! My God sent His angel, and He shut the mouths of the lions. They have not hurt me, because I was found innocent in His sight.'"
~ Daniel 6:21-22

Remember Mary who, with all of God's people, had been waiting for the Messiah for thousands of years? Look what God did!

"The angel answered and said to her, 'The Holy Spirit will come upon you, and the power of the Most High will overshadow you; for that reason also the holy Child will be called the Son of God.... For nothing will be impossible with God.'"
~ Luke 1:35, 37

Remember the disciples who were waiting behind closed doors in the days that followed Jesus' death? Look what God did!

"But God raised Him from the dead, freeing Him from the agony of death, because it was impossible for death to keep its hold on Him."
~ Acts 2:24

Of all the "impossibles" in the Bible, *this* is the one that altered the course of our lives forever! The only "impossible" for God was that death couldn't win. It wasn't possible for us to save ourselves or change our lives and secure our salvation. Only the One who has woven together the most amazing story of all time could do that. And He did it, not only with the death of His Son, but with the resurrection.

I don't know what "impossible" you are facing today that you desperately want God to alter. Perhaps it's your job, your relationships, your health, or your finances. Rest assured, dear friend, that the Master Seamster is at work through it all. He is carefully measuring the days, trimming the unnecessary fabric, adding details we could have never imagined. It's not our job to grab the scissors out of His hand to start cutting or pull the needle from His hand and begin stitching. It is simply to watch Him, marvel at His handiwork, and *be still* while He makes the necessary alterations for our lives.

PRAYER

> Lord, I know I can grow impatient with the timing of things in my life. You not only are weaving a beautiful story for my life, but You are doing so in Your perfect timing. Help me to "be still" and allow You to have control over my life. Nothing is impossible for You, God! Amen.

REFLECTION

When have you doubted the Master Seamster's plans for your life?
What "impossible" in your life are you waiting on God to alter?

_____

_____

_____

_____

_____

The Saxophone on the Sidewalk

"Weeping may last through the night,
but joy comes with the morning."

~ Psalm 30:5

I t had been five years. FIVE. That seems like a significant number in terms of years I've survived on this earth without my son. Perhaps almost milestone-ish. I felt like this particular "heavenversary" demanded something significant. Some celebration. Some meaningful activity. Some planned-out remembrance.

But as time drew nearer to the actual day, I found myself weighed down with other things that demanded my time and energy. Before I knew it, the day was just around the corner. With no celebration. No meaningful activity. No planned-out remembrance. I felt frustrated with my circumstances and even more guilty, that I couldn't—or didn't—have the time to give this important day enough thought. I mean, I was the *mom*. Shouldn't I be more...with it?

The day before the big "anniversary," I had an opportunity to walk down to the beach. It was the perfect time to think and come up with a plan. But as my thoughts wandered all over the place, I heard a noise, other than the music coming from my AirPods. It was music... *live* music. I looked up from the sidewalk, across the street and saw a man on his second-story balcony, playing the saxophone. Removing one of my airPods, I could hear the music much more clearly. It was upbeat. Lively. Joyful.

And as I watched him, with a smile on my face, I realized that this might just be the first September 5th in many years that I wasn't dreading or merely trying to survive. That just like the saxophone music, I was feeling...pretty joyful. Not about losing Joe, but because I had a lot to be joyful about. There would be joy in getting to spend this significant day with my *husband* (I still love saying that word) and hearing him preach about the grace of God in worship. There would be joy in celebrating his birthday with family. There would be joy in family and friends who sent messages to say they were thinking of me. And there would be joy in sharing Joe's favorite candy—a Kit Kat—with my husband who would be thoughtful enough to have one waiting.

But most of all, there would also be joy for my son, whose faith became sight on this day, five years ago. That even though he lost his life on this earth, he gained eternity in heaven with Jesus. He experiences the true joy of being a child of the one true King, in the presence of our Savior.

Although Scripture is replete with verses about joy, none seems quite so out of place than Hebrews 12:2, which says,

> *"And it was for the JOY set before Jesus, that He endured the cross, scorning its shame, and sat down at the right hand of the throne of God."*

Think about that: What could have possibly been the *joy* set before Jesus? Intolerable suffering? Excruciating pain? Public humiliation? Unjustified death? It doesn't seem to make any sense. That is, unless you know the heart of the Father. The details of the plan might not have been joyful. But the plan itself would bring unending joy for God's people – and for our God who has loved us since the beginning of time. And didn't want to be separated from us any longer. The joy was that Jesus knew everything He would endure meant eternal life for those who believe. That He was fulfilling his Father's plan as the ultimate sacrifice for our sin. Because of this, there's not only forever joy for my son and all believers in Christ, but there's forever joy for those of us who are still on this earth, grieving with hope. We are living proof that though we've experienced the worst life could throw at us, God still gives us beauty instead of ashes, joy instead of mourning and a garment of praise instead of a spirit of despair (Isaiah 61:3).

Maybe you, like me, have experienced your share of "toilet on the sidewalk" moments, those truly awful life-altering experiences you never saw coming. Perhaps you've had some "recliner on the sidewalk" moments as well, where God has allowed seasons of rest and rejuvenation. But I encourage you today to also look for the "saxophone on the sidewalk" moments that God has placed in your life. Those moments where, despite the sadness and grief and pain, you can still find joy. And peace. And *hope*. Even on a sidewalk.

PRAYER

Lord, thank You for giving me moments of joy in the midst of sorrow. Thank You for the hope I have because of Your work on the cross. May that reality give me the strength I need to continue on this earthly journey, until that glorious day when I will be clothed in the righteous garment of praise forever in Your presence! Amen.

REFLECTION

Reflect on a "saxophone on the sidewalk" moment in your life. How can you still find joy even when you walk through hardships?

You Have to Go through It

"When you pass through the waters, I will be with you;
and when you pass through the rivers, they will not sweep over you.
When you walk through the fire, you will not be burned;
the flames will not set you ablaze."

~ Isaiah 43:2

Picture it: June of 1982. A campground outside of Yellowstone National Park. It was a cool, summer evening and our family (including several aunts, uncles and cousins) had just traveled to Pocatello, Idaho, for my youngest aunt's wedding. We were spending time together following the event and weren't expecting the thunderstorm that suddenly popped up while we enjoyed time in the great outdoors. There was a scramble for nearly twenty of us to dart into my uncle's pop-up camper in an effort to stay dry. As an adult, this would seem like a semi-nightmarish situation, but as a seven-year-old, I was enamored with the fact that we were all huddled together in the dimly-lit camper while the storm raged around us. Always able to make the best of any situation, my twin aunts quickly settled all of us rowdy cousins down with a rousing rendition of "Goin' on a Bear Hunt." In seconds, we were all patting our legs in a steady rhythm and repeating chants of "Goin' on a bear hunt….we're gonna catch a big one….we're not scared….what a beautiful day." Our "journey" took us out of the house, past the gate, through the wavy grass, across the wide river, and tromping through the mushroom patch. We squealed with delight as we knew we were getting closer to the deep, dark cave where the big, hairy, scary bear surely lived. But in each "place" we went, there was only one option. We could never go under it. Or around it. Or over it. We always had to go *through* it.

I remember in the hours and days and weeks after Joe died thinking I wouldn't be able to survive. The ache was so great, the pain in my chest so real and so deep that I often feared I would succumb to heart failure. I would lay awake for hours, fearful that if I fell asleep, I wouldn't wake up. How would I survive Christmas or his birthday or really any other day? I didn't have the slightest clue how to live five minutes or five months or five years without my child.

Which begs the question...how did I survive? Or really, how does *anyone* survive such great loss and trauma and continue to live? I wish I had an easy answer. Or a checklist of things to do. But the best advice I can offer is to quote the great bear hunt: "I had to go *through* it."

I didn't *want* to go through it. I remember shortly after the paramedics came to tell me those awful, awful words, "Ma'am, I'm so sorry, we did everything we could." I pleaded with God to rewind the last hour of my life. I begged Him to fast forward time to a place in time when the pain wouldn't be so all-consuming. But there was no avoiding the days of barely being able to eat or sleep. Or the days of walking around in that cloud of grief. Or the particularly hard days of trying to survive a holiday or a birthday. I knew the clock would keep ticking and I would, by the grace of God, get *through* it. And indeed, I have. It's been nearly six years and, here I am, sitting at a Starbucks, sipping a tea...and surviving.

Gratefully, I didn't get through it alone. God sent people to walk with me. He sent his Spirit to be my Comforter. Because of that, I was able to find my way through the wavy grass of loss and the mushroom field of grief and the wide river of overwhelming sadness and plain old missing my baby boy. I didn't get to fast-forward any amount of time to get there. It was day after day after awful day of simply going through it.

Maybe you can remember the days of simply struggling to get through and survive. Maybe you're walking that road right now. You might be lost in the tall wavy grass. You might be slogging your way through a field of mushrooms or barely keeping your head above water in the wide river. But there is good news: Remember that deep, dark cave? You don't even have to put one foot inside. That's never a place God would ever expect or ask us to go and face the big scary bear of death. That was a job reserved for His Son. He sent Jesus to go *through* life on earth and *through* death on a cross. We know Jesus would have rather gone over death or around it or under it, instead of going *through* it. He asked His Father, "If it be possible, let this cup pass from me...." (Matthew 26:39) and asked again in verse 42. But His Father's will was for His Son to go *through* the pain, the suffering, the humiliation, and ultimately death, so that He could walk into the deep, dark cave of hell and declare that He had been victorious over death and the devil. To declare that those things would not have the power to come after us, chase us down, and destroy us. And to declare that we would be able to claim His victory as ours.

Friends, that is the answer to how we can survive the absolute worst things in our lives. We have a Savior who overcame death and the devil to give us hope and life eternal. It's that hope that helps us put one foot after another each day and keeps us breathing and surviving.

Unlike the conclusion of the bear hunt, where we run screaming from the bear and hide in our bed with the sheets pulled over our heads, scared of how we'll survive if that bear follows us inside, we can now walk as confident believers...and even run, straight into the arms of Jesus.

PRAYER

> Lord, I would so much rather skip the pain I know I must walk though, but I know I don't walk alone. Send your Holy Spirit to walk with me. Send people to put their arms around me and share my pain. Thank you for sending Jesus to go through the most painful and unimaginable death, so that I could somehow count it as my gain. Help me keep putting one foot in front of the other, to keep running the race, until one day I am reunited with my loved ones, but more importantly, with You. Amen.

REFLECTION

Who has God sent in your life to walk through a difficult season with you? How can you be someone who walks alongside another experiencing the same journey?

_____

_____

_____

_____

_____

Acknowledgments

To my incredible husband, Jim: Yours is the voice I value above all others. Your encouragement, your advice, and your support made me believe publishing this book was even a reality. Thank you for your relentless pursuit of preaching the Gospel and helping me wrestle with the "why's" of Joe's death in a way that has brought me closer to God. The way you love me and our children is the greatest blessing of my life. I still marvel that God chose me to be your wife. You're my forever person!

To my beautiful daughter, Ella: I would not be here today if it wasn't for you. You were my reason to get out of bed each day and kept putting one foot in front of the other. You have brought me joy beyond *anything* I could imagine. You are the living embodiment of resilience in Christ and God's miraculous healing. Your faith and bold witness inspire me daily. I cannot wait to see you spread your wings and fly out into the world! Just make sure to come back. And hug me occasionally.

To my most amazing sister, Kristen: I am forever indebted to you for my birthday gift in 2022, which started this whole crazy book dream. Thank you for fearlessly walking with me through the depths of sorrow that only you've witnessed. Through your own struggles, your trust in God shines through you so beautifully. I have learned so much about godly love and commitment from you. Thank you for being the best godmama Joe could have ever had!

To my fantastic editing team, Carol, JoAnne, Christie: thank you for the countless hours spent adding commas, finding numerous mistakes and writing encouraging notes in the margins. I am blessed beyond all measure for having you in my life!

To countless family and friends who prayed relentlessly for me through my darkest days and walked alongside me: Thank you for being the hands and feet of Jesus when I needed it the most. You all made me a believer in the tremendous power of prayer.

To everyone who made the comment at one point or another that, "Someday you should write a book!": I am so humbled that you took time to read my blogs and encourage me.

To my precious Joe: Even though I only had you for fourteen years, I am incredibly grateful for your life. I will always hold on to our many talks, our laughs, our cries, and our discussions on faith. There is never a day that goes by that I don't miss you fiercely. One day I will hold you in my arms again and tell you all about the toilet on the sidewalk.

And finally, to my God: I would not have one word of significance to write if it wasn't for Your constant strength, love, and grace in my life. All glory, praise, and honor to YOU, now and forever. Amen.

Printed in Great Britain
by Amazon

55451376R00094